Cambridge Elements

Elements in Second Language Acquisition
edited by
Alessandro Benati
The University of Hong Kong
John W. Schwieter
Wilfrid Laurier University, Ontario

IMPLICIT LANGUAGE APTITUDE

Gisela Granena
Universitat Oberta de Catalunya

CAMBRIDGE
UNIVERSITY PRESS

CAMBRIDGE
UNIVERSITY PRESS

University Printing House, Cambridge CB2 8BS, United Kingdom

One Liberty Plaza, 20th Floor, New York, NY 10006, USA

477 Williamstown Road, Port Melbourne, VIC 3207, Australia

314–321, 3rd Floor, Plot 3, Splendor Forum, Jasola District Centre,
New Delhi – 110025, India

79 Anson Road, #06–04/06, Singapore 079906

Cambridge University Press is part of the University of Cambridge.

It furthers the University's mission by disseminating knowledge in the pursuit of
education, learning, and research at the highest international levels of excellence.

www.cambridge.org
Information on this title: www.cambridge.org/9781108714402
DOI: 10.1017/9781108625616

© Gisela Granena 2020

First published 2020

A catalogue record for this publication is available from the British Library.

ISBN 978-1-108-71440-2 Paperback
ISSN 2517-7974 (online)
ISSN 2517-7966 (print)

Implicit Language Aptitude

Elements in Second Language Acquisition

DOI: 10.1017/9781108625616
First published online: August 2020

Gisela Granena
Universitat Oberta de Catalunya

Author for correspondence: Gisela Granena, ggranena@uoc.edu

Abstract: It is a well-known fact that some adult second language learners learn more rapidly and/or to a higher level of proficiency than others. Some of these individual differences have been linked to differences in cognitive and perceptual abilities under the umbrella term of "language aptitude." The notion of language aptitude has undergone recent developments, one of which is the proposal that language aptitude includes cognitive abilities that involve implicit processes and that are advantageous in learning a language without awareness. This Element defines implicit language aptitude, examines tasks that can be used to measure implicit language aptitude, and provides an overview of relevant research in this area.

Keywords: implicit learning, explicit learning, language aptitude, individual differences, implicit memory, explicit memory

ISBNs: 9781108714402 (PB), 9781108625616 (OC)
ISSNs: 2517-7974 (online), 2517-7966 (print)

Contents

1 What Are the Key Concepts?

Identifying and understanding the factors that affect second or foreign language learning and that can predict rate of progress of acquisition and/or long-term achievement (i.e., ultimate attainment) has been one of the main areas of interest in the field of second language acquisition (SLA). Among the many individual differences that explain variation in second language (L2) learning outcomes, one that has attracted the attention of researchers since the 1950s has been language aptitude. "Language aptitude" is a catch-all, umbrella term to refer to cognitive and perceptual abilities that contribute to high achievement in language learning. In educational psychology, Cronbach and Snow (1977) used a broad definition of aptitude that included cognitive, affective, and conative (i.e., motivational) characteristics needed for achievement in a particular situation. Specifically, Snow (1991) defined aptitude as "any measurable person characteristic hypothesized to be needed as preparation for response to treatment to successful goal achievement in the treatment(s) studied" (p. 205). According to this definition, aptitude can include characteristics of the individual such as abilities, skills, previous knowledge, beliefs, attitudes, and motivation. In applied linguistics, however, the use of the term "aptitude" is more restricted. As DeKeyser and Koeth (2011) explain, the term is mostly limited to cognitive aspects of an individual that are relatively stable and largely determined by genetics and early experience. These cognitive aspects are considered good predictors of language learning and language processing holding equal all other factors such as motivation and other individual differences, which are also meaningful in the context of language learning (Doughty et al., 2010).

It is well-established that the nature of language aptitude is componential or, in other words, that aptitude is a complex of abilities. DeKeyser and Koeth (2011) suggested speaking of "cognitive aptitudes," in the plural, for learning an L2, rather than "language aptitude," and pointed out that any aptitude test would have to measure these various aptitude components. The problem is that the nature of these components is not so well-established and, as a result, researchers are still trying to put together all the pieces regarding the theoretical constructs that are relevant components of aptitude for L2 learning and processing and regarding the type of contribution they make to language learning.

The late 1950s and 1960s saw much research on language aptitude. This research, conducted under government auspices, aimed at developing measures that could predict rate of progress of language learning and that could be used for placement and selection purposes in language programs by government agencies or other organizations. Government agencies, international organizations such as the World Bank, and missionary organizations are some of the organisms that are interested in selecting employees for language aptitude in order to assign them an appropriate language to learn in terms of difficulty level (Stansfield & Winke, 2008). Fruit of this interest in aptitude in the 1950s was the creation of the Modern Language Aptitude Test battery (MLAT; Carroll & Sapon, 1959), the most well-known and most widely used measure of aptitude to date. In the 1960s, Pimsleur created the Pimsleur Language Aptitude Battery (PLAB; Pimsleur, 1966) and, in the 1970s, the US Department of Defense created the Defense Language Aptitude Battery (DLAB; Petersen & Al-Haik, 1976). The objective they all had in common was to achieve as much predictive validity as possible. Predictive validity is the ability of an instrument to predict some other variable, usually in the future. To create the MLAT, for example, the widest possible variety of cognitive tests that could be valid predictors of success in learning foreign languages was selected (Carroll, 1958). There was no theory of aptitude guiding the selection of tests (a language aptitude model was only proposed by Carroll, 1962, a posteriori, based on the empirical results of the project). In addition, "success" in learning was operationalized as course grades and these grades were mostly based on written tests and daily quizzes. Considering that the audio-lingual method was the most popular teaching methodology at the time, it is not surprising that the cognitive ability with the greatest predictive validity was rote memory. Other abilities that showed good predictive validity were also related to different types of memory (e.g., associative memory). As a result, four of the five subtests in the MLAT (Number Learning, Phonetic Script, Spelling Clues, and Paired Associates) measure different aspects of memory. Undoubtedly, written tests and quizzes involve much memory work, but it is arguable whether being good at language learning is simply a matter of memory. It is arguable as well whether obtaining good course grades means being competent in an L2, understanding by competence not only grammatical competence, but also ability for use.

From a practical perspective, the MLAT succeeded as a predictor of rate of progress in the foreign language classroom (i.e., language learning in the short run). According to the MLAT manual, predictive validity was generally high with coefficients ranging between 0.25 and 0.83, according to Pearson's r. However, the test was not created to predict L2 learning in the long run (i.e., ultimate attainment) or high-level (i.e., advanced) L2 learning. Also, from a theoretical perspective, the approach taken may be criticized for being too myopic, since the test did not effectively reflect the theoretical domain to which it was related. After the MLAT was published, Carroll (1962) proposed an aptitude model, which he developed in a bottom-up fashion from the battery of approximately twenty cognitive tests that were initially used to derive the final five MLAT subtests. The model had four components: phonetic coding ability (codifying, assimilating, and recalling phonetic material), rote memory (ability to recall words in an unfamiliar language), grammatical sensitivity (identifying grammatical functions of words or phrases in sentences), and inductive language learning ability (figuring out the rules of systematically varying language materials). Three of these components are measured by the MLAT. Inductive language learning ability was measured in the initial battery of tests, but it was not included as part of the final five-test battery. Carroll's definition of the theoretical domain of language aptitude was made before a series of rapid developments in the neighboring field of cognitive psychology. These advances in human cognitive abilities contributed to the understanding of language aptitude in applied linguistics and to a refinement of the definition of the theoretical domain. Two main areas of rapid development since the 1950s that have influenced the conceptualization of aptitude in SLA have been the areas of human memory and implicit learning.

Regarding the area of implicit learning, a key concept in this Element, research started in the late 1960s when the term "implicit learning" was introduced by Reber (1967) in a report on artificial grammar learning. The report described studies showing that learning without awareness was possible, something that is ubiquitous in the real world, the clearest example being language acquisition and socialization during infancy, but which was considered a novel finding in the context of a research laboratory at the time. Reber's research in the 1960s was carried out parallel to Chomsky's research program on a genetically determined universal grammar that was innate and that served as the basis for all language acquisition (e.g., Chomsky, 1965). Reber aimed at capturing and showing the learning process behind language acquisition in the laboratory in order to address the learnability problem that Chomsky solved with the notion of a universal grammar. In the laboratory, Reber used artificial grammar tasks, an experimental paradigm that investigates implicit learning, defined as "learning in the absence of intention to learn and in such a way that the acquired knowledge cannot be easily verbalized" (Cleeremans, Allakhverdov, & Kuvaldina, 2019, p. 1). In artificial grammar tasks, participants are asked to observe or memorize a series of symbol strings. These strings follow a complex set of rules. Then, in the testing phase, participants are asked to classify novel symbol strings as grammatical or ungrammatical, depending on whether they follow or violate the rules that controlled the structure of the symbol strings participants saw in the acquisition phase. Since the 1960s, implicit cognition has been an ever-growing field, further spurred by the research on implicit memory and its neurocognitive underpinnings in the 1980s (Schacter, 1987; Schacter & Graf, 1986; Squire, 1992). However, theory and empirical findings in this area remain controversial.

At the theoretical level, defending two simultaneous but qualitatively different, or separate, learning systems, explicit (i.e., conscious, analytical, effortful, and slower) and implicit (i.e., nonconscious, holistic, effortless, and faster), is a view consistent with dual-process or dual-system theories of higher cognition (e.g., Epstein, 1990, 2008; Evans & Over, 1996; Stanovich & West, 2000; Witteman et al., 2009). According to these theories, implicit and explicit cognition are architecturally and evolutionarily different and involve two different modes of processing, automatic and controlled. Dual theories have been challenged by researchers who view the distinction between implicit and explicit as continuous (e.g., Dienes & Perner, 1999) and who propose a single-system continuum of thought requiring different levels of consciousness from explicit to implicit. Also, in terms of language learning, it is a matter of debate whether adult learners can learn an L2 implicitly. Bley-Vroman (1990, 2009) proposed the Fundamental Difference Hypothesis, according to which there is a qualitative difference between the learning mechanisms of child and adult L2 learners. The hypothesis, as formulated in 1990, stated that the implicit learning mechanisms that operate in child language learning are no longer efficient in adult language learning and that domain-general problem-solving mechanisms are used instead, a position supported by DeKeyser (2000), who also predicted that adults would need high verbal analytic ability to succeed in L2 learning. Meisel (2009) further claimed that the fundamental differences in learning mechanisms between child and adult acquisition may already emerge in early childhood, earlier than the critical age range hypothesized by Bley-Vroman (1990) (i.e., end of teens), and only for certain grammatical properties.

Although alternative theories have been suggested (e.g., DeKeyser, 2007), there is evidence supporting that the capacity for implicit learning weakens, but does not disappear, by age twelve (Hoyer & Lincourt, 1998; Long, 2017, citing Janacsek, Fiser, & Nemeth 2012). In addition, the findings of experimental studies that have focused on adult learners' implicit learning of semi-artificial grammars (Rebuschat, 2008; Rebuschat & Williams, 2006, 2009; Williams, 1999, 2005) typically show 65 percent accuracy in implicit learning groups, versus chance performance in control groups. If the capacity for implicit learning weakens, this makes it possible for cognitive aptitudes for implicit learning to compensate for the loss in efficiency of implicit learning mechanisms. The decline in the efficiency of implicit learning mechanisms could have a greater impact on the acquisition of certain language features and, as a result, a relationship between the acquisition of these features and individual differences in aptitude for implicit learning would become apparent.

At the level of empirical research, providing evidence in support of implicit learning processes is challenging. If the evidence is based on learning outcomes (i.e., acquired knowledge measured during a testing phase of an experiment), these outcomes can be the result of implicit learning, explicit learning, or a combination of both. Alternative experimental paradigms such as the serial reaction time (SRT) have been proposed (Nissen & Bullemer, 1987) that allow measuring learning online (i.e., during the training phase) using reaction time data. Evidence of implicit learning may be also indirectly established by measuring the extent to which participants are aware of the acquired knowledge, in (semi-)artificial grammar learning studies, even though the existence of verbalizable knowledge does not necessarily imply that learning did not happen implicitly, since implicitly acquired language knowledge (e.g., one's native language) can become verbalizable to a lesser or greater extent. Finally, evidence of implicit learning may be also indirectly established by linking learning outcomes with selected cognitive aptitudes that were engaged in during the learning process, as suggested by DeKeyser (2012).

Behind the claim that there is an aptitude for implicit learning, lies the assumption that individual differences of this trait exist at the population level. However, according to Reber's earlier work (e.g., Reber, 1989, 1993), individual differences in implicit learning should be minimal, relative to individual differences in explicit cognition, due to the fact that implicit learning is evolutionarily older and reflects primitive cognitive systems. The issue of individual variation in implicit learning is of considerable theoretical and practical importance. Theoretically, Reber's (1993) evolutionary theory of implicit learning predicts that this type of learning preceded the development of explicit cognition, which did not develop until *Homo sapiens*. As a result, the theory predicts fewer individual differences than in conscious processes, which are more recent in terms of evolution, and a dissociation with performance on standard psychometric measures of intelligence, which engage explicit cognitive processes. Practically, if there is no variation in implicit learning, this means that the general population is homogenous in this regard and that implicit learning cannot covariate with or be meaningfully related to other variables. In his later work (e.g., Reber & Allen, 2000), however, Reber conceded that individual differences in implicit functioning do exist, based on empirical findings showing measurable differences in both implicit rule learning and incidental learning. The existence of individual differences solved the practical problem without affecting Reber's evolutionary theory, since any measurable differences in implicit functioning can still be predicted to be on a tighter distribution than differences in explicit functioning and to be largely independent from differences obtained on explicit measures.

Subsequent research in cognitive and educational psychology provided further evidence in support of the existence of individual differences in implicit learning. Kaufman et al. (2010) and Woltz (2003) both showed individual differences in implicit cognition and defended the idea that implicit learning is a cognitive ability. Kaufman et al. (2010) investigated the implicit learning of sequential patterns via the SRT procedure, an experimental paradigm where participants are asked to respond as quickly as possible to a series of nonverbal stimuli (e.g., asterisks) that appear at specific locations on a computer screen. The order of locations is either dictated by a complex set of rules or is a repeating sequence. In both cases, participants typically show a decrease in reaction times, suggesting that they have learned to anticipate the location of the stimuli. Kaufman et al. provided evidence of individual differences on a probabilistic SRT task as well as evidence of meaningful relations between performance on the SRT task and areas of complex cognition, such as verbal analogical reasoning and educational attainment in a variety of domains, including foreign language. They concluded that this was an area deserving further study. Woltz (2003) argued that individuals can be expected to differ in implicit cognitive processes, just as they differ on most cognitive measures, and provided evidence of individual differences in repetition priming (i.e., the ability to process stimuli faster without conscious guidance or intention when they are repeatedly presented) and semantic priming (i.e., the ability to make subconscious meaning associations). Woltz further suggested that the general domain of implicit cognitive processes could be a fruitful area in which to investigate new aptitude constructs, arguing that exploring individual differences in implicit learning could result in aptitude constructs that have minimal overlap with existing ones, which in general involve explicit, declarative processes.

These calls for new aptitude constructs in educational psychology (e.g., Woltz, 2003) and cognitive psychology (e.g., Kaufman et al., 2010) have led to a re-examination and re-conceptualization of language aptitude in the SLA field that departs from the old constructs of the first aptitude test batteries such as the MLAT. There is no doubt that implicit cognitive abilities constitute a fruitful area to investigate new aptitude constructs. There is no doubt either, as this Element will try to convey, that implicit cognitive abilities constitute a challenging area to investigate due to the elusive nature of implicit cognitive processes and to the fact that implicit cognitive abilities have failed to yield evidence of a unitary construct (e.g., Gebauer & Mackintosh, 2007; Siegelman & Frost, 2015).

This introduction has aimed at providing an overview of the key concepts surrounding the notion of language aptitude and the proposal that language aptitude includes cognitive abilities involving implicit processes, such as implicit learning and implicit memory, which are advantageous to learning an L2 without awareness. Sections 2, 3, and 4 of this Element will delve into the notion of implicit language aptitude and its measurement and provide a focused overview of relevant research studies investigating individual differences in implicit learning and memory and their role in L2 learning.

2 What Are the Key Readings?

2.1 Definition of Implicit Language Aptitude

Implicit language aptitude can be defined as those cognitive abilities that facilitate implicit learning and processing of an L2, understanding by "implicit" "in the absence of (1) conscious intention to learn, (2) conscious awareness of the fact that we are learning, and (3) conscious attribution of any noticed change to the effects of learning" (Jimenez, 2002, p. 62). Implicit cognitive abilities rely on selective attention (i.e., attention directed to the relevant dimensions of the input), but do not engage central executive resources like explicit abilities (see Table 1 for a comparison of implicit and explicit mechanisms on a number of dimensions). As Jimenez (2002) puts it, implicit learning "does not depend on the intention to learn or directly on the amount of attentional resources available, it crucially depends on whether learners selectively attend, or respond in any way, to the relevant stimulus dimensions" (p. 59). In other words, selective attention, but not executive attention, is required for implicit learning. Once stimuli are selectively attended, with relatively low-level perceptual attention, implicit learning can occur automatically without engaging any additional executive processing resources.

Table 1 Characteristics of explicit and implicit cognitive mechanisms (from MacDonald, 2008, p. 1013)

Implicit system	Explicit system
Not reflectively conscious	Conscious
Automatic	Controllable
Fast	Relatively slow
Evolved early	Evolved late
Parallel processing	Sequential processing
High capacity	Limited by attentional and working memory resources
Effortless	Effortful
Evolutionary adaptation or acquired by practice	Acquisition by culture and formal tuition

Proposals to include implicit cognitive abilities as part of language aptitude (Granena, 2013a; Linck et al., 2013) were made in an attempt to refine and expand the prevailing concept of language aptitude in SLA. These proposals were made following calls for new aptitude constructs in educational and cognitive psychology (Woltz, 2003; Kaufman et al., 2010). For decades, the understanding of language aptitude in SLA had been shaped by early aptitude test batteries such as the MLAT (Carroll & Sapon, 1959), the Pimsleur Language Aptitude Test Battery (PLAB; Pimsleur, 1966) and the Defense Language Aptitude Battery (DLAB; Petersen & Al–Haik, 1976). These batteries have in common the fact that they were developed for placement or selection purposes having predictive validity in mind. They also have in common the fact that they are biased toward measuring cognitive abilities in the explicit domain. These are abilities that depend on intentional processes that require conscious monitoring and that rely on executive functions such as shifting, updating, and inhibition, all centered in the prefrontal cortex, a late-developing area of the brain in terms of evolution. The cognitive abilities that have been most commonly measured as part of language aptitude, largely as a result of the influence of the MLAT, have been rote memory and language analytical ability, two abilities that predicted learning outcomes under popular teaching methods at the time the MLAT was created, such as the audio-lingual method.

Rote memory, or explicit associative memory, has been measured via paired associates learning tasks, which present a series of stimulus–response associations for participants to memorize. MLAT V measures this ability via twenty-four words in an unknown language with their corresponding English translations for participants to memorize in two minutes. Participants are then asked to provide the translation of the words. Language analytical ability has been measured via tests such as MLAT IV, Words-in-Sentences, which asks participants to identify the grammatical role of highlighted parts of sentences. Carroll (1962, 1981) made a distinction between the ability to recognize the grammatical function of a word (i.e., grammatical sensitivity) and the ability to induce the rules governing a set of language materials. However, Skehan (1989) considered both abilities different aspects of language analytical ability, an ability that can be considered to overlap with metalinguistic ability (Ranta, 2008) and with explicit inductive learning ability, since tests such as the Words-in-Sentences provide participants with data and guidance so that they focus on structural properties of language and derive their understanding of a grammatical feature.

As a result of the influence of the early aptitude test batteries, aptitude to learn a language meant being able to memorize and consciously reflect on linguistic structure. This view of aptitude was not aligned with how languages are learned under contemporary teaching approaches that adopt task-based or other experiential approaches (Long & Doughty, 2009). Approaches such as task-based language teaching (Long, 2017) emphasize meaning-based communication rather than formal aspects of the target language. These advances in the understanding of how languages are learned, together with advances in the fields of cognitive and educational psychology, led to the need to update the concept of language aptitude in the SLA field and to the development of new aptitude measures (i.e., the Hi-LAB; Linck et al., 2013) that included cognitive abilities from both the explicit and implicit domains.

As already brought up in Section 1 of this Element, claiming the existence of an implicit type of language aptitude raises questions regarding the possibility to learn an L2 implicitly, even in adulthood, and regarding the existence of individual differences in implicit abilities and their meaningful relationship with other factors, including language learning outcomes. As for the possibility to learn implicitly, much of the foundational experimental work on this topic can be attributed to the pioneering research of Arthur Reber (e.g., Reber, 1993). The earliest studies on the acquisition of complex patterns without awareness were conducted in the 60s using artificial grammar learning experiments (e.g., Reber, 1969; Reber & Millward, 1965, 1968). These experiments showed that adult participants developed some sensitivity to the constraints of the grammar through exposure to exemplars and that they were able to acquire patterns of sequential dependencies. Implicit learning was seen as a "generalized, domain-free inductive process that derives information about patterned relationships in the stimulus environment, and represents these relationships in an abstract and tacit form" (Winter & Reber, 1994, p. 117). In the SLA field, this line of research has inspired the work by N. Ellis (e.g., Ellis, 1996) and the claim that L2 acquisition is driven by sequence learning or chunking, a type of learning that is highly sensitive to items that co-occur at greater than chance levels in the input. According to this view, learners progress from the use of memorized formulaic phrases through slot-and-frame patterns to more open grammatical constructions (e.g., Ellis & Cadierno, 2009). Other experimental studies that have focused on adult learners' implicit learning of semi-artificial grammars (Rebuschat & Williams, 2006, 2009; Williams, 1999, 2005) typically show 65 percent accuracy in implicit learning groups, versus chance performance in control groups. These findings suggest that the capacity for implicit learning is not lost in adult learners (see, e.g., Long, 2017), even though it deteriorates and weakens with age (Hoyer & Lincourt, 1998; Janacsek, Fiser, & Nemeth, 2012). Although there is evidence of implicit learning in the literature, there is risk of certain circularity in the definition of a so-called implicit language aptitude (i.e., *petitio principii*), since what is to be proved is already assumed in the premises, thus creating a circle in reasoning. Effective measures of implicit cognitive abilities are needed, as well as validation studies of available measures.

A well-known challenge that implicit learning studies have to face when they rely on learning outcomes (i.e., acquired knowledge) is that these outcomes can be the result of implicit learning, explicit learning, or a combination of both. As the *polarity fallacy* referred to by Reber (1993) says, one should not treat implicit and explicit learning as completely independent, since they complement each other and cooperate. They are not all-or-none processes, but graded processes. Defending the existence of implicit learning does not deny the interaction between learning and consciousness or the fact that learning can lead to the adoption of explicit strategies. Even the fact that knowledge can be verbalized does not necessarily imply that learning did not happen implicitly, since implicitly acquired language knowledge (e.g., one's native language) can become verbalizable to a lesser or greater extent. In the end, the notion of learning is precisely distinguished from the broader concept of adaptation because it operates on cognitive representations that are accessible to consciousness (Jimenez, 2002). Experimental studies can, nevertheless, balance explicit and implicit elements. They can also rely on online measures of learning and provide indirect evidence of implicit learning either by measuring the extent to which participants are aware of the acquired knowledge or by establishing a relationship between learning outcomes and cognitive aptitudes (DeKeyser, 2012).

Regarding the existence of individual differences in implicit abilities, Reber (1993) hypothesized that there should be little individual variation, and less than in explicit processes, due to the fact that implicit learning mechanisms are evolutionarily older and, therefore, more robust. The assumption that implicit learning is characterized by a tight distribution at the population level has, however, been challenged by research showing that individual differences in implicit memory and learning do exist. For example, Woltz (1990a, 1990b, 1999) demonstrated that implicit memory measures of priming had reliability estimates high enough (internal consistency > 0.60) to suggest measurable individual differences. In addition, these individual differences do have correlates in other spheres of cognition and personality. As a result, implicit cognitive processes can be considered abilities with meaningful individual differences. As for the cognitive correlates of implicit learning ability, Kaufman et al. (2010) reported a significant correlation with processing speed, but no relationships between implicit learning and general intelligence scores, intentional associative learning, or working memory. Similarly, Woltz (1990a, 1990b, 1999) found that differences in priming were unrelated to measures of general intelligence. Several studies converge on showing a dissociation between individual differences in implicit learning and individual differences in working memory (e.g., Feldman, Kerr, & Streissguth, 1995; McGeorge, Crawford, & Kelly, 1997; Siegelman & Frost, 2015; Unsworth & Engle, 2005) and between individual differences in implicit learning and individual differences in general intelligence (e.g., Gebauer & Mackintosh, 2007; Reber, Walkenfeld, & Hernstadt, 1991; Robinson, 2005; Siegelman & Frost, 2015). Individual differences in implicit learning have been further related to other forms of complex cognition. Woltz (1990a, 1990b, 1999) reported a relationship between priming ability and reading ability. Kaufman et al. (2010) reported a relationship between implicit learning ability and academic achievement in foreign language, and Pretz, Totz, and Kaufman (2010) a relationship between implicit learning and both math and language achievement. Similar relationships have been reported by studies using other measures considered to tap implicit processes, such as artificial grammar learning. Misyak and Christiansen (2012) and Conway et al. (2010) focused on L1 abilities and found correlations between performance in an artificial grammar learning task and L1 reading comprehension (Misyak & Christiansen, 2012) and sensitivity to word predictability in L1 speech perception (Conway et al., 2010).

Regarding the personality correlates of individual differences in implicit learning, Kaufman et al. (2010) found a significant correlation with the intuition facet of the Myers–Briggs Type Indicator (MBTI; Myers et al., 1998) and with the Openness aspect of the Big Five (DeYoung, Quilty, & Peterson, 2007) domain Openness/Intellect, where Openness reflects engagement with sensory and perceptual information and Intellect reflects intellectual engagement. Kaufman et al. (2010) further showed that while Openness predicted implicit learning ability, Intellect did not, and while Intellect predicted working memory, Openness did not, indicating a double dissociation in their data. They argued that individuals characterized by the Openness trait may be more engaged with the perceptual world, which may facilitate implicit learning, or may have a wider focus of attention, which may help with the unconscious detection and learning of covariance structures. Intuition was also related to implicit learning in a task involving hidden covariation detection in Woolhouse and Bayne (2000), where participants had to judge the job suitability of a series of candidates based on a personality profile, where suitability was determined by a nonsalient rule concerning the scores. Granena (2016) found that measures of aptitude hypothesized to tap more explicit cognitive processes were associated with scores on the rationality scale of the Rational-Experiential Inventory (REI; Pacini & Epstein, 1999), an inventory that measures different cognitive approaches to information processing and in which the rationality scale is used to identify individuals who like analyzing and thinking logically. On the other hand, performance on the probabilistic SRT learning task was associated with experientiality, a scale that identifies individuals that tend to look for the big picture, read between the lines (intuiting), and rely on memory and associations. Also using the REI, Witteman et al. (2009) showed that rationality scores were strongly and significantly correlated with performance on a series of logical problems, vignettes, and the jelly bean task, while experientiality scores were negatively correlated.

In the field of SLA, research is still scarce but there are several studies that have found a relationship between implicit cognitive abilities and L2 learning outcomes. These studies will be reviewed in section 4 of this Element.

2.2 Constituents of Implicit Language Aptitude

Implicit language aptitude is not a unitary construct, but rather a multifaceted construct with multiple constituents. Different measures of implicit cognitive ability have not been shown to load on a common factor (e.g., Gebauer & Mackintosh, 2007), even though there is enough overlap among them to suggest a shared source of variance (e.g., Kalra, 2015). Kalra, Gabrieli, and Finn (2019) tested a one-factor model using scores from four different tasks (artificial grammar learning, probabilistic classification, SRT, and implicit category learning) as indicators. While the model with these four tasks revealed poor fit, a model without the artificial grammar learning scores revealed good fit. Kalra et al (2019) argued that, given that the artificial grammar learning paradigm includes a learning phase and a test phase where participants are asked to judge whether a stimulus is grammatical, the task may be biased toward explicit processes. Alternatively, they argued that the underlying mechanism serving artificial grammar learning could be implicit but quite different from that underlying the other three tasks, as several neuropsychological studies seem to suggest (e.g., Reber et al., 2003).

A factor to consider when investigating whether implicit learning is a unitary ability is modality. All the tasks in Kalra et al. (2019) were visual. Siegelman and Frost (2015), however, analyzed a battery of statistical learning tasks in the visual and auditory modalities and could not find evidence of a unified statistical learning capacity. They reported low correlations between the different tasks, indicating different mechanisms of statistical learning or different patterns of learning depending on the characteristics of the stimuli. Further subdivisions are likely to be needed, but a first broad distinction can be made in implicit language

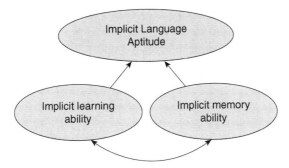

Figure 1 The construct of implicit language aptitude: a model

aptitude between implicit inductive learning ability and implicit memory ability (see Figure 1).

The most recent aptitude test battery in the SLA field, the High-Level Language Aptitude Battery (Hi-LAB; Linck et al., 2013) included a set of eleven tests measuring cognitive and auditory perceptual abilities grouped into six different constructs. Two of these constructs, long-term memory retrieval and implicit learning, rely on abilities in the domain of implicit cognitive processes. Long-term memory retrieval is measured by a semantic priming task (i.e., ALTM synonym) showing subconscious meaning associations (i.e., the ability to activate semantic networks in an unconscious way), whereas implicit learning is measured by a SRT task showing subconscious pattern-learning (i.e., the ability to pick up on patterns without needing to think about them consciously). Also, in a study that explored the underlying structure of a group of tests from two different aptitude test batteries, the Hi-LAB (Linck et al., 2013) and the LLAMA (Meara, 2005), Granena (2019) reported two factors related to implicit cognitive abilities that were interpreted as implicit inductive learning ability and implicit memory ability. Implicit inductive learning ability was defined as the ability to pick up patterns after experiencing them in the input without having to think about them consciously (for example, without knowing the rules behind, without searching for information, or without building/testing hypotheses). Implicit memory ability was defined as the ability to retain and retrieve information effortlessly and incidentally. The semantic priming task from the Hi-LAB measuring long-term memory retrieval and the sound recognition subtest LLAMA-D from the LLAMA loaded together on a separate factor from a SRT task measuring implicit learning. Granena (2019) argued that, even though LLAMA-D is a recognition task, and recognition tasks are supposed to involve episodic (explicit) memory retrieval, recognition can also be based on the assessment of stimulus familiarity (Yonelinas, 2002). That is, recognition can be based on the sensation that an item has been seen before without explicitly remembering any detailed contextual information. Given that familiarity-based recognition memory judgments have been shown to rely on the same process that supports conceptual implicit memory (e.g., Wang & Yonelinas, 2012), Granena (2019) argued that both LLAMA-D and the long-term memory retrieval task from the Hi-LAB were measuring implicit memory.

Implicit memory is a term that is intimately related to implicit learning because there can be no learning without memory and there can be no memory in the absence of learning. This explains why a task such as the SRT task is referred to in the literature mostly as a measure of implicit learning (e.g., Kaufman et al., 2010), but can also be found as a measure of procedural (i.e., implicit) memory (e.g., Hamrick, 2015). In order to distinguish between implicit learning and memory, it is necessary to refer to the three stages of memory: encoding, maintenance, and retrieval. Implicit learning focuses on the encoding stage (i.e., the acquisition of knowledge), while memory focuses on the maintenance (i.e., storage) of knowledge in a state than can be retrieved at a later time (Squire, 1987). Implicit memory involves, therefore, the effortless, incidental retrieval of known information, acquired either incidentally or intentionally, whereas implicit learning is the incidental acquisition of new knowledge without awareness. Retrieval in the case of implicit learning could be either intentional, if the participant became aware of the learned material after learning took place, or incidental, if the participant did not become aware of the learned material, case in which accuracy- or reaction time–based performance measures would have to be used.

In the case of implicit memory, it is helpful to distinguish between different types of implicit memory in the context of the multiple memory systems theory (e.g., Squire, 1987). Neuroscientists agree that long-term memory is not unitary. Squire (1987, 1992) identified a declarative and a nondeclarative memory system, each relying on a different long-term memory store. Declarative (or explicit) memory referred to the capacity of conscious recollection about facts and events. It is generally available to awareness and verbal report and it is the type of memory that is impaired in amnesic patients. It is the memory system that supports "knowing that" (i.e., memory for information, either for events, episodic memory, or knowledge about the world, semantic memory). Nondeclarative (or implicit) memory, on the other hand, is an umbrella term encompassing several additional memory systems and it refers to memory that is accessed without consciousness, or implicitly, through performance rather than recollection. It is the memory system that supports "knowing how." While declarative memory depends on the medial temporal lobe, nondeclarative memory depends on multiple brain systems outside of the medial temporal lobe (Squire & Zola-Morgan, 1991). Evidence of such separation of memory systems comes from studies showing that depth of encoding of an item does not affect repetition priming, but does affect explicit memory for that item (Graf, Mandler, & Haden, 1982). Conversely, matching perceptual input modality, whether auditory or visual, between encoding and retrieval at the test stage affects repetition priming, but not explicit memory for an item (Jacoby & Dallas, 1981).

Nondeclarative memory includes several forms of implicit memory abilities. Squire and Zola-Morgan (1991) distinguished between procedural, associative, nonassociative, and priming. These distinctions are important, first, because these different systems are dissociable from declarative memory and from each other and, second, because different implicit memory tasks will be tapping one system or another. It should also be clarified that one of these implicit memory systems, procedural memory, can be used to refer to acquisition, and has been used to mean implicit learning (see Morgan-Short et al., 2014). These researchers accept an overlap between implicit learning and the acquisition stage of procedural memory (i.e., the acquisition of procedural knowledge) and, as a result, investigate the effect of individual differences in procedural learning ability on L2 syntactic development using cognitive measures of procedural learning, such as the Tower of London task (Shallice, 1982), which this Element will review in the next section. While it is true that procedural memory is memory for skills and habits, and that skill learning that relies on this memory system can sometimes occur nonintentionally (i.e., without a declarative phase; see Knowlton, Siegel, & Moody, 2017), the notion of procedural learning understood according to Anderson's (1987) skill learning theory is incompatible with the notion of implicit learning understood according to Reber (1993), because Anderson's skill learning requires an initial declarative stage, while Reber's implicit learning requires acquisition that takes place without awareness. These differences in the understanding of procedural learning and the fact that skills can be acquired in the absence of awareness under some circumstances, but are generally amenable to explicit learning strategies (Squire, Knowlton, & Musen, 1993), is important, because some of the cognitive tasks proposed to measure procedural learning (or procedural memory acquisition) may not qualify as measures of implicit learning in the Reberian sense.

Much of the empirical evidence for implicit forms of memory comes from priming studies. Generally speaking, priming refers to performance facilitation that can be attributed to a single prior processing event, but with no recall or recognition of it. For example, an individual is more likely to complete the word "str_" with "ong" than with "eet" if they had previously been exposed to the word "strong." This characteristic distinguishes priming from other types of implicit memory that also result in facilitation, because priming results in facilitation due to a specific prior event, while other types of implicit memory, such as procedural memory, result in facilitation due to multiple and related prior events. There are different types of priming, each relying on a different type of cognitive mechanism: repetition priming, further subdivided into perceptual priming and conceptual repetition priming, and semantic priming. Repetition priming involves a processing event that is identical or practically identical to the target performance event. The events can be nearly identical in physical form and structure, such as the words "boat" and "goat" (perceptual priming) or in terms of meaning, such as "soggy" and "wet" (conceptual repetition priming). Semantic priming is very similar to conceptual repetition priming because the prior processing event resembles the target event in semantic features but, unlike conceptual priming, it does not contain identical semantic content and does not require repetition of exactly the same semantic process. For example, in a lexical decision task where participants have to decide whether an item is a word or not, the processing of the word "steak" will be faster when it follows a semantically related prime word such as "food."

To summarize, the structure of implicit language aptitude has not been systematically explored in research and, therefore, remains largely unknown. A broad distinction can be made between implicit learning ability and implicit memory ability. However, because the difference between learning and memory tasks depends on whether the focus is placed on the encoding stage or on the maintenance and retrieval stage, tasks assessing these abilities have been used interchangeably to refer to implicit learning and procedural memory. A type of implicit memory ability is priming ability. Priming tasks assess an individual's primability and some of them (i.e., repetition priming tasks) have been claimed to measure the elemental processes of procedural memory, specifically those that underlie longer-term skill learning (i.e., the early stages of proceduralization; Gupta & Cohen, 2002; Poldrack & Gabrieli, 2001).

2.3 Measurement of Implicit Language Aptitude

The implicit cognitive domain is a complex one. Measuring implicit cognitive abilities is challenging, not only because of long-standing debates regarding whether a task can be considered fully implicit, but because, in comparison to their explicit counterparts, implicit tasks typically present lower reliability indexes. For example, Granena (2013b) reported a reliability of 0.44 for a probabilistic SRT task, using split-halves with Spearman-Brown correction. Kaufman et al. (2010) also reported a reliability of 0.44 and considered it standard for probabilistic SRT tasks, on the basis of the reliability of implicit learning in the literature (Dienes, 1992; Reber et al., 1991; Robinson, 1997).

Reber et al. (1991), and Robinson's (1997) replication study, reported split-half reliabilities of 0.51 and 0.52, respectively, also using the Spearman-Brown correction. The lower reliability indexes of implicit tasks indicate that they are noisier, probably as a result of the fact that they place fewer constraints on performance and tend to rely on change scores. As explained by Woltz (2003), imposing greater processing constraints on a task helps increase reliability – for instance, setting specific performance goals and avoiding multiple solutions for an item, since these can involve different cognitive processes and lower reliability. Nevertheless, acceptable reliability indexes have also been reported for implicit measures. Kalra (2015), for example, reported moderate test-retest reliability indices for a SRT task, a category-learning task, and a probabilistic classification task.

Rather than the reliability of assessment for implicit learning and possible ways to increase it, which future studies should definitely address, the main source of controversy concerning implicit tasks has been the claim that they involve explicit processes. This is why the same cognitive task can have different versions that attempt to increase its validity. For example, the SRT task (Nissen & Bullemer, 1987) has deterministic, alternating, and probabilistic versions. In the deterministic version, the same ten- or twelve-element-long sequence is presented repeatedly to participants and this sequence is combined with a random sequence that forms the baseline against which to measure the difference in reaction time. This version has sometimes been criticized as potentially allowing for the use of explicit strategies (e.g., Shanks & Johnstone, 1999), even though specific features of the deterministic version itself, such as the number of repetitions of the sequence before the introduction of the random sequence, response-to-stimulus interval length, or sequence length (i.e., whether the sequence has fewer or more elements) can minimize explicit learning. In the alternating version (Howard & Howard, 1997), random stimuli are alternated with predetermined stimuli resulting in a probabilistic structure in terms of high-frequency (i.e., typically over 60 percent) and low-frequency sequences of three trials (or triplets).

The probabilistic version (e.g., Kaufman et al., 2010) relies on conditional probabilities in an attempt to recreate the noisy conditions where implicit learning typically takes place. Trials are congruent with a target sequence 85 percent of the time. The rest of the time, trials are congruent with an alternate sequence. These two sequences exclusively differ in the second-order conditional information they convey. Reed and Johnson (1994) gave the sequences of three locations the name of *second order conditionals* (SOCs) (vs. first-order probabilities, where the location of an item is unambiguously predicted by the preceding item with a probability of 1.0). In second-order conditionals, at least two locations are needed to predict the next location in the sequence. In other words, knowing the previous location alone provides only limited information regarding the next location.

In what follows, a compendium of cognitive tasks is provided and a summary of the tasks is displayed in Table 2. As explained below, whether each of these tasks is actually a measure of the specified construct will ultimately depend on a number of task specificities that vary depending on the version of the task that is administered and that research shows can have considerable impact in the case of implicit cognition. The implicit learning literature further shows that it is even hard to find significant correlations among different tasks measuring the same type of learning (e.g., Siegelman & Frost, 2015). For example, auditory and visual statistical learning tasks and even auditory statistical learning tasks with verbal (natural) or nonverbal (synthesized speech) stimuli did not show any correlations in Siegelman and Frost (2015) and they did not correlate with a SRT task either, despite all being considered measures of implicit learning ability. This indeed raises a critical theoretical question for future research avenues.

2.3.1 Artificial Grammar Learning Task (Reber, 1967)

This task consists of a training, or exposure, phase and a testing phase. In the training phase, participants view a series of unpronounceable and meaningless letter strings on a computer screen (e.g., MXRMXT, VMTRRR). These strings are generated by a Markov grammar, a finite-state system where each subsequent event depends probabilistically on the current event. All letter strings are grammatical (i.e., positive exemplars). Participants are asked to memorize the strings.

After the training phase, participants are told that there was a grammatical system underlying the strings. Then, they are asked to judge whether a series of letter strings (all new) are grammatical or ungrammatical according to this system. Specifically, they are asked to choose whether the string comes from the same set of rules as the words they saw during the training phase or not. Grammatical and ungrammatical strings are matched for length and chunk strength to avoid competing explanations that could account for participants' correct endorsement of grammatical items. Chunk strength is a measure of the frequency with which the components of a string in units of two or three consecutive letters occurred on average during the training phase. Participants are also asked to verbalize the rules of the underlying system. The expected result is no correlation between accuracy and reportable grammar knowledge. That is, participants should be able to discriminate grammatical from

Table 2 Implicit language aptitude tasks

	Implicit language aptitude tasks		
Task name	Abbreviation	Measures	SLA studies
Artificial Grammar Learning	AGL	Endorsement rate of grammatical items (abstract learning) Endorsement rate of high chunk strength items (concrete learning)	Kim & Godfroid (2019)
Visual Statistical Learning	VSL	Mean score (correct identifications) Mean reaction time	Brooks et al. (2017)
Auditory Statistical Learning	ASL	Mean score (correct identifications) Mean reaction time	
Serial Reaction Time	SRT	Mean raw reaction time difference Median raw reaction time difference Single block score	Granena (2013b, 2019), Granena & Yilmaz (2019a), Hamrick (2015), Linck et al. (2013), Maie (2019), Suzuki & DeKeyser (2015, 2017)
Weather Prediction	WP	Total percentage accuracy	Morgan-Short et al. (2014, 2015)
Tower of London	TOL	Mean reaction time (before and/or after first move) Mean number of moves Mean number of trials in minimum number of moves	Morgan-Short et al. (2014, 2015)
Synonym Available Long-Term Memory	ALTM	Residual difference scores	Granena (2019), Linck et al. (2013)
A/Not A Prototype-Distortion Category Extraction	CAT	Total percentage accuracy	

ungrammatical strings above chance levels, but should be unable to verbalize the rules used to generate the strings.

Artificial grammar learning has been criticized as a measure of implicit learning on several grounds (see Kaufman et al., 2010), which explains why the task has undergone many modifications (e.g., Berry & Dienes, 1993; Cleeremans, Destrebecqz, & Boyer, 1998). One reason is that participants are explicitly instructed to memorize strings. Another reason is that the task includes separate training and testing phases, and that, at the testing phase, participants are typically informed of the existence of an underlying structure. Other criticisms relate to how participants are asked to report grammar rules, since it may be too difficult for them to report their knowledge (Dulany, Carlson, & Dewey, 1984).

2.3.2 Visual Statistical Learning Task (Frost et al., 2013)

This popular test of statistical learning (see also Emberson, Conway, & Christiansen, 2011; Glicksohn & Cohen, 2013; Kirkham et al., 2002; Turk-Browne, Junge, & Scholl, 2005) employs a sequential stream of meaningless shapes with adjacent contingencies. It measures participants' ability to pick up regularities in the visual modality. It includes a familiarization phase, followed by a test phase. Participants are exposed to twenty-four abstract shapes presented in a consecutive stream for about ten minutes. Shapes are organized into eight triplets with transitional probabilities between shapes within triplets of 1, as the second shape always follows the first, and the third always follows the second. The test phase in Frost et al. (2013) consisted of two-alternative forced-choice items including a triplet that appeared in the stream and a triplet with shapes in an order that did not appear in the stream (i.e., transitional probability of 0). Participants' success rate in identifying the original triplets is interpreted as their ability to learn transitional probabilities implicitly. Several variants of this task have been proposed.

Bertels, Franco, and Destrebecqz (2012) proposed increasing the difficulty of the task by including variability in transitional probabilities so that they are not always 1 and introduced a cover task asking participants to respond to the presentation of black letters displayed within the sequence of shapes. Cover tasks give a task to do while watching and, thus, help prevent participants from learning intentionally and from passively viewing the stream without paying selective attention (Turk-Browne et al., 2005). In addition, Bertels et al. (2012) included direct and indirect measures of learning, a four-choice completion task where participants had to decide on the missing shape, and a rapid serial visual presentation task, in order to determine how aware participants were of the learned information. Binary confidence judgments were added to every item on the completion task indicating whether they guessed or felt that their response was based on some recollection of the learning material. Confidence judgments are used to apply two common criteria in the implicit learning literature (Dienes et al., 1995). The first one is the guessing criterion (Cheesman & Merikle, 1984): if participants claim to guess but their performance is above chance level, then they are not aware of the knowledge they acquired. The second one is the zero-correlation criterion (Chan, 1992): if participants are more confident in their correct responses than in their errors (i.e., incorrect responses), then they are aware of the knowledge they acquired.

Bertels et al. (2012) reported evidence of both explicit and implicit knowledge acquisition for those participants who performed above chance on the completion task (i.e., participants who demonstrated learning). These participants indicated that they were more confident in their correct responses than in their errors, suggesting that at least part of their knowledge was explicit. At the same time, their answers were correct even when they claimed to be guessing, indicating that their performance was at least partly dissociated from confidence level and that they were at least partly unaware of the knowledge they acquired (but see Tunney & Shanks, 2003, regarding participants' bias to claim that they are guessing when they are not). Conversely, one third of the participants demonstrated learning on the indirect measure (i.e., they were faster to react to the third position in the triplets of the rapid serial visual presentation task), despite performing at chance in the four-choice completion task. In other words, they acquired knowledge but could not apply it to completion performance. Bertels et al.'s (2012) results questioned the sensitivity of direct methods of assessment of statistical learning and challenged previous findings claiming that visual statistical learning is exclusively based on unconscious knowledge acquisition.

Siegelman, Bogaerts, and Frost (2016) also proposed a version of the visual statistical learning task that aimed at making the task more sensitive to individual differences. They considered the reliability scores of the task reported in the literature as mediocre: test–retest reliability was $r = 0.58$ and split-half reliability was 0.64 (Siegelman & Frost, 2015). They claimed that a weakness of the task is that in many studies a large proportion of the sample performs at chance level. In general, studies report on mean group performance to show that is significantly above chance, but do not report on the percentage of participants exhibiting learning significantly above chance[1]. If a large proportion of

---

[1] Siegelman et al. (2016) suggest looking at the binomial distribution and calculating how many trials a participant needs to answer correctly in order to determine whether a participant's score is significantly above chance ($p < 0.05$). For example, for a two-alternative forced-choice task with thirty-two trials, significant above-chance performance corresponds to twenty-two correct answers or more. An online tool to run binomial tests was found here: http://users.abo.fi/jtuo main/speech/z_score.html

participants perform at chance, those are data points reflecting noise and their predictive validity is compromised. They proposed that a good test of individual differences should have a large number of test items in order to discriminate adequately. They also suggested that the number of repeated items should be minimal to prevent participants from relying on episodic memory of the previous response they provided. Unlike Bertels et al.'s, Siegelman et al.'s task only included direct measures of learning (a completion and a recognition test) and did not include a cover task during the exposure, or familiarization, phase. As a result, conscious knowledge acquisition cannot be discarded.

2.3.3 Auditory Statistical Learning Task (Siegelman et al., 2018)

This is the auditory counterpart of the visual statistical learning task described in the previous section and it belongs to a well-established paradigm (e.g., Saffran et al., 1997). Like its visual counterpart, it includes an exposure and a test phase. During the exposure phase, participants listen to an unsegmented stream (i.e., not including any word boundaries) composed of tri-syllabic nonsense words. Within the language stream, the transitional probabilities within words are higher than between words. Participants are told that they will be hearing a monologue in an unfamiliar language. The test phase includes a recognition task where participants hear two words (tri-syllabic sequences) and have to decide which belongs to the unfamiliar language. In addition to direct measures of learning, other studies such as Batterink et al. (2015) and Franco et al. (2015) also rely on indirect measures of learning (e.g., target-detection tasks) that assess whether participants are able to process predictable targets more efficiently on the basis of faster reaction times.

A factor to consider when administering the auditory statistical learning task is participants' first language. Siegelman et al. (2018) argued that, compared to tasks with nonverbal auditory sounds or visual tasks with material such as abstract shapes, performance on auditory-verbal tasks may be influenced by participants' native language and the expected speech co-occurrences depending on their native language (i.e., prior knowledge).

2.3.4 SRT Task (Nissen & Bullemer, 1987)

In this nonverbal task, implicit learning of a sequence is measured online (i.e., during the training phase). The task requires a motor response and this is why it has sometimes been considered a simple motor-skill learning task. However, there is research showing that sequence learning can be supported by purely perceptual learning when the motor sequence is removed (Dennis, Howard, & Howard, 2006). In the SRT paradigm, a visual cue can appear at any one of four positions, which are horizontally arranged on a computer screen and which correspond to a different button on a response pad. Participants react to the continuous visual sequence of stimuli by selecting the appropriate response button as fast and accurately as possible, as in a normal reaction-time paradigm. Participants are not informed that the sequence of stimuli follows a pattern. The sequence, typically ten or twelve items long, can be deterministic or probabilistic. Blocks of random stimuli or a new sequence are inserted toward the end to assess sequence learning and distinguish it from general practice effects. In the deterministic SRT, the sequence is a fixed-length string of events that plays out repeatedly. In the probabilistic SRT, which also includes the alternating SRT (Howard & Howard, 1997), there are probabilities governing the transition between the events. To ensure implicit learning, the time between the events, the response-to-stimulus interval (RSI), should be kept relatively small, or should be eliminated, since explicit learning can take place even if participants are just given 250 or 500-msec to think (Destrebecqz & Cleeremans, 2001).

The measure of interest can be derived in different ways. Usually, it is computed as the difference in reaction time (i.e., milliseconds) between random and sequence trials. In the deterministic version, the mean reaction time in the last sequence block is compared to the mean reaction time in the immediately following random block. This difference score can be further divided by the mean reaction time in the last sequence block in order to express the difference score as a percentage. Other times, the difference between the average of the mean reaction times across random blocks and the average of the mean reaction times across sequence blocks is derived and divided by the random average. In the probabilistic version, the average response time on probable trials is subtracted from the average response time on improbable trials. Error responses have to be discarded (but reported), as well as outlier responses that are +/- 3 standard deviations from the mean, computed individually for each block and participant.

Typically, response time decreases as sequence learning takes place (e.g., Willingham, Nissen, & Bullemer, 1989). This learning is considered implicit as subjects perform poorly in recalling the structure of the sequence in recognition tests administered at the end of the entire session (e.g., Destrebecqz & Cleeremans, 2001). On these tests, participants are told that the stimuli they saw were sequenced. They are usually asked to provide confidence ratings to old and new short sequences on a Likert-scale, for example, from 1 ("I am sure that this sequence was part of the test") to 6 ("I am sure that this sequence was <u>not</u> part of the test"). If participants are unable to discriminate old from new, this supports the claim that learning was implicit, since it shows that there is no conscious access to sequence knowledge. However, as Shanks and Johnstone (1999) point out, if partici-pants are able to discriminate old from new, this could be due to the unconscious misattribution of fluency to oldness. In other words, participants may become aware of the fact that some of their responses are faster and judge those sequences as more familiar. That is the reason why, if discrimina-tion is possible, Shanks and Johnstone suggest comparing reaction times of sequences judged old and new, independently of actual old–new status, to test whether there is a contribution of explicit sequence memory to recognition performance over and above the fluency factor. Explicit knowledge can also be assessed with a series of "generate tasks" (e.g., Nissen & Bullemer, 1987; Destrebecqz & Cleeremans, 2001; Willingham et al., 1989). In these tasks, participants are given parts of the sequence and required to predict the following position or positions by pressing the correct buttons.

These tests can be combined. For example, prior to "generate tasks," a free recall phase may be added to be used as validity check by asking participants to explicitly recall any parts of the sequence they had encountered, or similar questions, to evaluate degree of awareness. Granena (2013b) also combined a recognition test with a generate task in order to have subjective and objective elements to compare. Participants were required to predict the third position in a series of triads from old and new sequences and, then, they were asked to provide a confidence rating between 1 and 6, with 6 being the most confident that the sequence did not appear in the training phase.

2.3.5 Weather Prediction Task (Knowlton, Mangels, & Squire, 1996; Knowlton, Squire, & Gluck, 1994)

This is a forced-choice probabilistic category-learning task. Participants have to predict rain or sunshine on the basis of geometric patterns (cues) that are probabilistically associated with each of the two weather outcomes. Specifically, participants see one to three out of four different cue cards and they are asked to classify each of the sets into rain or sunshine. Cue combina-tions, or patterns, are probabilistically associated with each weather outcome. As a result, participants have to learn which outcome is more probable given a particular pattern. For example, a card of squares, a card of circles, and a card of pentagons may represent a 75 percent chance of rain. Feedback is provided on each trial.

Typically, participants begin performing at chance level (50 percent cor-rect) and they end choosing the most associated outcome around 70 percent of the time. They are unable to articulate the probabilities, but nevertheless tend to predict weather outcomes more accurately as they gain more experience with the task. Categorization accuracy (also referred to as "optimal responses"), both over all the trials and block by block, and response speed are usually calculated.

Some researchers have argued that learning on the weather prediction task relies mostly on explicit processes and that it can solved with a high accuracy rate by relying on explicit strategies (e.g., Price, 2009). Others claim that learning on this task is based on simple rule-based strategies, but only initially (Gluck, Shohamy, & Myers, 2002). Participants can apply explicit learning strategies by learning associations between two stimuli (cue card and outcome). This can happen because either they use a one-cue strategy (i.e., decide on the basis of the presence/absence of a particular cue card on a set) or focus on those trials where only one cue card is presented and respond by chance on the rest of trials that include more than one card. Instead, the use of multi-cue strategies, a process of gradual learning over many trials in which participants take the combination of all cue cards into account, is considered to reflect procedural learning on this task. This is usually defined as the improvement of response accuracy across all the trial blocks.

In order to minimize reliance on explicit strategies, dual-task versions of the weather prediction task can be used (Foerde, Knowlton, & Poldrack, 2006). For example, Morgan-Short et al. (2014) included a secondary task that consisted of asking participants to count the number of high tones heard during a trial while making the weather prediction.

2.3.6 Tower of London Task (Shallice, 1982)

In this task, participants see a board with upright sticks and three balls of different colors arranged in a start position and another board with the same upright sticks and balls arranged in a goal position. Participants are asked to match the goal configuration and rearrange the colored balls by transferring them one at a time, usually in a specified number of moves. The test involves looking ahead in order to determine how to move the colored balls on the sticks. Different performance variables of interest can be identified. The time taken to complete the pattern, the total number of moves needed, as well as the number of trials performed in a minimum number of moves are usually calculated as measures of participants' planning ability. Some studies distinguished between time taken to make first moves (defined as planning) and time taken to complete the task thereafter (defined as execution; e.g., Gangopadhyay et al., 2018). Morgan-Short et al. (2014) calculated a learning measure based on "initial think time," operationalized as the time between the beginning of a trial and the first move made by the participant, independent of whether the trial was solved in the specified number of moves. Then, they derived a proportional change in think time by subtracting the reaction time of the first trial from the reaction time of the final trial and dividing the result by the reaction time of the first trial. Typically, the results show improved performance. Efficiency progressively increases as the number of moves per trial decreases and speed increases.

However, whether this can be interpreted as evidence of implicit learning (or procedural memory acquisition) is subject to debate. This test makes substantial demands on executive functions. Participants need to strategize a plan and they are actually encouraged to plan their steps before making the first move. Planning is a complex process that involves (a) inhibitory control, in order to avoid making excessive (or wrong) moves, (b) updating, in order to be able to maintain the rules of the task, and (c) task-switching, in order to be able to switch among subgoals or moves. Working memory should be clearly contributing to tower performance (e.g., Phillips et al., 1999). Although this task does not seem to qualify as a measure of implicit learning in the Reberian sense, some researchers (e.g., Peretti et al., 2002) have used it to measure procedural, skill learning according to Anderson's (1987) ACT theory of skill acquisition, since the two stages involved in the Tower task, the learning-to-solve stage and the problem-solving routine stage, can be identified with the two stages in Anderson's model: a first stage where progressively more accurate explicit strategies are acquired with practice, and a second stage in which practice makes the problem-solving process more efficient and reliable with a faster and smoother execution.

The tower task has different versions. In addition to the tower of London, there is the tower of Hanoi (Simon, 1975) and the tower of Toronto (Saint-Cyr, Taylor, & Lang, 1988). The tower of London and the tower of Toronto are simpler versions of the tower of Hanoi, since colors are easier to perceive than sizes, the tower of Toronto being of intermediate difficulty. The tower of Hanoi includes three different-colored disks and the additional rule that a larger disk can never be placed on top of a smaller disk. The tower of Toronto includes four different-colored disks and the additional rule that one cannot move a darker disk onto a lighter one.

2.3.7 ALTM Synonym Task (Linck et al., 2013)

This test, from the Hi-LAB aptitude test battery, measures semantic or associative priming, or the extent to which the activation of one concept in participants' lexicon will activate related concepts, thus indicating facilitation of lexical processing. Stimuli on this test are, therefore, verbal and language-specific

(English). The test includes two tasks. In the priming task, participants listen to a list of five words. Then, they are shown two topic words, one of which is a synonym for two of the words in the list and one of which is a synonym for the other three words in the list. For example, a participant can hear *moist smart damp brilliant soggy*, where three words are synonyms of "wet" and two words are synonyms of "intelligent" (Was & Woltz, 2007). Participants' task consists in indicating the word that had more synonyms in the list by answering a question such as "Were there more words meaning wet or intelligent?" In the comparison task, participants see pairs of words and their task is to indicate whether the meanings of the words are similar or different. There are eighteen sets in the comparison task, each of which comes after a priming list from the priming task. Each set includes twelve word pairs, four of which are unscored and eight of which are scored. Nine of the sets are primed and nine are unprimed. In primed sets, one or both words in the pairs are synonyms of one of the two topic words from the priming list (e.g., "wet" or "intelligent"). In unprimed sets, none of the words are synonyms of the two topic words from the preceding priming list.

A rate score combining response time and accuracy for each comparison was computed. The score shows correct responses per minute and it results from dividing the number of correct responses in a set by the total response time within that set. Separate scores for same and different comparisons within each of the nine primed sets are computed. These rate scores within each primed set are then regressed on the corresponding unprimed set. This yields a residual priming score that captures variability in the rate score of primed sets (i.e., dependent variable) that is left over after accounting for the variability explained by the rate score of unprimed sets (i.e., independent variable). The eighteen residual difference scores resulting from same and different comparisons within the nine primed sets are added to create the final score. A positive score means more priming and a negative score, less priming.

A factor analysis reported in Granena (2019) showed that the ALTM synonym task loaded together with one of the subtests in the LLAMA aptitude test battery (Meara, 2005), LLAMA-D. LLAMA-D is a sound recognition task where test-takers have to discriminate between old and novel items. Recognition is usually associated with episodic (explicit) memory retrieval, but it could also be familiarity-based (Yonelinas, 2002). This means recognition based on the sensation that an item has been experienced before without explicitly remembering any detailed contextual information. Familiarity-based recognition memory judgments have been shown to rely on the same process that supports conceptual implicit memory (e.g., Wang & Yonelinas,

2012). There is also evidence that familiarity is mediated by some of the same regions that mediate repetition priming (e.g., Thakral, Kensinger, & Slotnick, 2016). Based on these findings, Granena (2019) argued that LLAMA-D could also be tapping implicit memory ability.

2.3.8 Prototype-Distortion Category Extraction (Fried & Holyoak, 1984)

In this task, participants are asked to classify visual nonverbal stimuli into a category. Category exemplars are created by randomly distorting a category prototype. Typically, a constellation of seven or nine black dots forms the category prototype and exemplars are created by randomly distorting the spatial location of each dot. There are different versions of this task. In "A/B" versions, two prototypes are created and participants are asked to classify a number of exemplars (e.g., 50) from each category. In "A/Not A" versions, a single prototype is created and participants are presented with exemplars that belong to that category or random patterns. There is some evidence (e.g., Heindel et al., 2013; Zaki et al., 2003) indicating that these two versions engage different memory systems. A/B prototype extraction has been claimed to engage the declarative memory system, since exemplars from two categories are presented along with feedback in each trial allowing participants to learn on the basis of trial-and-error. In this case, participants cannot rely on the abstraction of a central tendency.

A/Not-A prototype extraction, however, has been claimed to engage nondeclarative memory, particularly priming. In this version of the task, exemplars from a single category are presented during a training phase without reference to a subsequent testing phase to avoid that participants intentionally try to remember. Participants are simply instructed to point to the center dot in each pattern. After the training, they are informed that the patterns they had seen belonged to a single category and that during the test they will have to determine which patterns also belong to that category. Because participants were only exposed to exemplars from one category during the training, they can base their category membership decision on similarity (or familiarity) criteria and, thus, rely on implicit memory during the test. Some of the evidence in support of these two dissociable versions of the same task comes from amnesic patients who show normal performance on A/Not-A prototype extraction, but impaired performance on A/B prototype extraction (Zaki et al., 2003). Another dissociation reported in the literature with patients with Parkinson's disease is between performance on A/Not-A prototype extraction and probabilistic category-learning tasks such as the weather prediction task (e.g., Keri, 2003).

3 What Are the Main Branches of Research?

This section of the Element will review studies in the field of SLA that have investigated individual differences in implicit cognitive abilities as predictors of L2 learning outcomes, either in naturalistic or instructed SLA contexts. In cognitive and educational psychology, implicit cognitive abilities have been meaningfully related to complex cognition and personality. For example, Gebauer (2003) found that implicit learning as measured by a battery of tasks correlated significantly with academic achievement in math and foreign language learning. Kaufman et al. (2010) found that implicit learning on a probabilistic SRT task was independently related to academic performance in foreign language learning. Also, holistic, impulsive, and experiential cognitive profiles (i.e., individuals who tend to look for the big picture, read between the lines, and rely on intuition) have been positively related to cognitive abilities in the domain of implicit cognition. Specifically, self-reported preference for intuition on the Myers–Briggs Type Indicator (MBTI; Myers et al., 1998) and for openness to experience, a related construct, in the NEO personality inventory (Costa & McCrae, 1992) were both significantly and positively correlated with implicit learning in a probabilistic SRT task (Kaufman et al., 2010). Similar results were reported by Granena (2016) using structural equation modeling. In the study, self-reported ability on the experiential-intuitive scale of the Rational-Experiential Inventory (REI; Pacini & Epstein, 1999) was significantly related to performance on Kaufman et al.'s (2010) probabilistic SRT task. The experiential cognitive style is characterized by intuitive, holistic thinking and it is fast, primitive, associated with emotionality and creativity, and it develops through life experiences (Epstein, 1994, 2008). These results suggest that individuals who prefer to rely on a more holistic, or nonanalytical, approach to information processing are better at learning complex patterns in the environment implicitly. As Kaufman et al. (2010) argue, these individuals "may be more open to implicit learning since their selective attention will focus on a wider variety of stimuli, and thus be more likely to capture relevant associations" (p. 336).

However, the relevance of individual differences in implicit cognitive abilities in SLA will be ultimately determined by their predictive utility in relation to L2 learning outcomes. It is expected that implicit cognitive abilities facilitate the acquisition of patterns in the input unintentionally during L2 exposure by gradually accumulating associations between frequently co-occurring features. Specifically, individuals with greater implicit cognitive abilities could have an advantage at picking up patterns without needing to think about them consciously in naturalistic, or immersion, contexts which maximize the opportunities for implicit learning by providing massive input or in implicit learning conditions of L2 instruction. These individuals could also have an advantage at learning complex (nonsalient or subtle) language aspects that are difficult to notice. Although this area is largely unexplored in SLA, there are some recent findings consistent with these claims.

Research on implicit cognitive aptitudes is highly relevant for SLA since it contributes to the explicit/implicit debate within SLA. Research on implicit and explicit learning is considered of critical value to the study of SLA (Hulstijn, 2005). On the one hand, this research can throw light on the differential degree of success in L2 learning, compared to L1 acquisition, an issue of major theoretical value. On the other, this research can inform materials designers, curriculum planners, and teachers about the benefits of the implicit and explicit learning modes.

3.1 Implicit Language Aptitude in Naturalistic L2 Learning

Empirical studies on the role of implicit cognitive abilities in naturalistic L2 learning contexts where learners are immersed in the L2 are very scarce. Two studies that have examined implicit language aptitude in this context have looked at implicit abilities as a predictor of long-term achievement with participants who are very advanced or near-native speakers of the L2. Granena (2013b) investigated implicit sequence learning ability as measured by the probabilistic version of the SRT task (Kaufman et al., 2010) in early and late learners' morphosyntactic attainment in L2 Spanish. The study was motivated by DeKeyser's (2000) proposal of a link between cognitive abilities and underlying learning mechanisms. Specifically, DeKeyser (2000) predicted that cognitive abilities that play a role in explicit language learning should be necessary for late L2 learners to reach a high level of L2 attainment because they learn predominantly through explicit mechanisms. Building on this argument, Granena (2013b) hypothesized that if implicit language learning mechanisms are still available in adulthood, even if they are less efficient, there should be a relationship between individual differences in implicit cognitive aptitudes and L2 attainment in adult learners. The study measured morphosyntactic attainment by means of an untimed grammaticality judgment test with a metalinguistic knowledge component that allowed controlled use of L2 knowledge, and a word monitoring task (Marslen-Wilson & Tyler, 1980) that required automatic use of L2 knowledge. Results showed that performance on the probabilistic SRT task moderated late L2 learners' attainment in the case of structures involving grammatical agreement as measured by the word monitoring task, a task hypothesized to tap integrated, implicit language knowledge, but not as measured by the metalinguistic knowledge test, a test where late L2 learners might have relied on additional explicit knowledge and analytic, metalinguistic skills. Granena (2013b) concluded that findings were consistent with the claim that the capacity for implicit learning is not lost in adult L2 learners (see, e.g., Rebuschat & Williams, 2009; Williams, 2005), although it deteriorates with age (Hoyer & Lincourt, 1998).

Suzuki and DeKeyser (2015) investigated the extent to which an SRT task predicted L2 performance on an elicited imitation and a word-monitoring task. The main goal of the study was to probe the validity of elicited imitation and word monitoring as measures of implicit L2 knowledge by comparing performance on these two tasks with performance on a SRT task. If the knowledge tapped by a task is implicit, this knowledge may have been acquired at least partly through implicit learning mechanisms, which are the mechanisms that the SRT task taps into. As a result, a relationship between the two may be expected. Similarly to Granena (2013b), the study included a total of sixty-three L2 learners (L1 speakers of Chinese) who were residents in the L2-speaking country, Japan. The study compared participants with longer and shorter lengths of residence in the L2 environment (nineteen versus forty-two month, respectively). A long length of residence was operationalized as thirty months or longer and a short length of residence as less than thirty months. Results showed a moderate positive relationship in the long-length-of-residence group between SRT task scores and grammatical sensitivity on the word monitoring task. In this group, elicited imitation scores did not correlate with word monitoring scores, but they correlated with metalinguistic knowledge test scores. In the short-length-of-residence group, SRT task scores and word monitoring scores were not related, but elicited imitation scores also correlated with metalinguistic knowledge test scores. Metalinguistic knowledge and word monitoring were not related in either of the two groups. Suzuki and DeKeyser (2015) concluded that their findings supported word monitoring as a measure of implicit knowledge, but that only L2 learners with sufficient L2 exposure seemed to be able to draw on implicit knowledge on this task. Their findings, however, failed to support elicited imitation as a measure of implicit knowledge and indicated that it was rather a measure of explicit knowledge.

In a subsequent study with 100 L2 speakers of Japanese, Suzuki and DeKeyser (2017) explored whether explicit knowledge facilitates the acquisition of implicit knowledge (i.e., the so-called interface problem) in a naturalistic L2 acquisition context. In addition to L2 measures of implicit and explicit knowledge, the study included measures of explicit and implicit aptitude. Like in Suzuki and DeKeyser (2015), a SRT task was used as a measure of implicit aptitude. Using structural equation modeling, the authors showed that automatized explicit knowledge significantly predicted the acquisition of implicit knowledge (i.e., interface position). However, there were no effects of implicit aptitude on the acquisition of either automatized explicit or implicit knowledge, even though the coefficient for the path from the SRT task to implicit knowledge was larger than the path from the SRT task to automatized explicit knowledge, which was interpreted as suggesting that the learners had not completely lost the capacity to learn implicitly. A limitation of the study was that the three implicit knowledge measures used (word-monitoring, self-paced reading, and visual-world tasks) did not correlate with one another. The only significant correlation was between word-monitoring and self-paced reading, a result that Suzuki and DeKeyser attributed to factors such as the variability that characterizes measures based on reaction time and eye tracking and to characteristics of the learners' profile, such as their length of residence, which ranged between two and sixteen years.

Further research is clearly needed in this particular area, but the three studies reviewed provide some evidence in support of the relevance of implicit cognitive ability, particularly the SRT task, as a factor to consider in naturalistic learning contexts in order to explain the learning outcomes of L2 learners with extensive language experience in the L2-speaking country.

3.2 Implicit Language Aptitude in Instructed L2 Learning

Empirical studies on the role of implicit cognitive abilities in instructed (experimental or nonexperimental) L2 learning contexts are also scarce, but this learning context seems to have attracted the attention of SLA researchers more than the naturalistic context. One of the reasons could be the potential of experimental research designs in this area to provide indirect evidence of the type of processing under different instructional interventions (DeKeyser, 2012). A positive association between a cognitive factor and learning under a specific condition suggests that the mental processes that are engaged by the instructional condition are facilitated by the value of the learner's specific cognitive ability. For example, a relationship between performance on the SRT task and learning outcomes in an instructed condition considered to be implicit would suggest that learning under that instructional option was also implicit. As already discussed, this type of evidence has major theoretical implications for SLA, since notions of implicit and explicit learning have been involved in explanations of the differential success of L2 acquisition compared to L1 acquisition (e.g., Bley-Vroman, 1990, 2009; DeKeyser, 2000).

One of the first studies that included measures of implicit language aptitude such as the SRT to predict L2 learning outcomes in an instructed setting was Linck et al. (2013). The main goal of the study was to find cognitive predictors of successful L2 learning at advanced proficiency levels. To address this goal, Linck et al. (2013) developed the Hi-LAB, a battery of cognitive tests that could predict language learning advantages at advanced stages of SLA, unlike previous aptitude batteries such as the MLAT, designed to predict advantages in the initial stages of SLA. Participants were United States federal employees from US government agencies and the US military and their proficiency level was determined by means of the Defense Language Proficiency Tests (DLPT; Defense Language Institute Foreign Language Center, 2009) and/or through job performance. The Hi-LAB battery included eleven computer-delivered tests of domain-general[2] cognitive abilities and specific perceptual abilities. The tests measured six main constructs: working memory (including executive functioning –updating, inhibitory control, and task-switching and phonological short-term memory), explicit associative memory, long-term memory retrieval, implicit learning, processing speed, and auditory perceptual acuity. In the study, highly proficient L2 learners were compared with a mixed-attainment group of learners that varied considerably in their proficiency level. The study focused on listening and reading skills. The test measuring implicit learning ability was a SRT task adapted from Willingham, Nissen, and Bullemer (1989) with higher scores indicating better sequence learning. The results showed that implicit learning ability was a predictor of both listening and reading attainment together with the paired associates and the letter span tasks, measures of explicit associative memory and phonological short-term memory, respectively. Specifically, implicit learning ability showed the strongest coefficients in the listening analysis, providing support to the hypothesis of the study that language aptitude, as measured by the Hi-LAB, would relate to listening abilities more strongly than to reading abilities.

Using tests of the same aptitude battery, the Hi-LAB, in addition to the LLAMA aptitude tests, Granena (2019) explored their potential as predictors of L2 speaking proficiency, operationalized in terms of complexity, accuracy, and fluency. A total of 135 college-level learners of L2 Spanish in the United States participated in the study. The results showed that the ALTM Synonym

---

[2] A domain-general cognitive ability refers to a general mental capability, a basic mental process, for example, problem solving, which can predict performance in various areas. Intelligence, executive functioning, attentional control, or speed of processing would be all considered domain-general cognitive ability factors. A domain-specific factor in the case of mathematical ability would be a competence such as quantity understanding, number recognition, or counting, which only predict mathematical skills. In the case of language ability, phonological processing would be a domain-specific factor.

test from the Hi-LAB measuring long-term memory retrieval in combination with the LLAMA-D subtest (sound recognition) were able to predict L2 fluency measured as pruned speech rate per minute. Granena argued that the ALTM Synonym test and LLAMA-D were measures of implicit memory tapping the ability to retrieve previously learned information effortlessly and incidentally. As Woltz (2003) pointed out, some individuals are better at spreading activation in implicit memory and at making use of information more efficiently. The fact that individual differences in implicit memory were related to variation in L2 speed fluency in Granena (2019) suggests that implicit memory ability may help L2 learners build meaningful word associations and recall words more quickly and automatically. The ALTM Synonym measure, however, was not a significant predictor in Linck et al. (2013). Granena (2019) attributed this to the fact that Linck et al. examined reading and listening skills (i.e., receptive language use), and not speaking skills. Implicit memory ability could be a more relevant ability for productive language use because production requires actual language retrieval.

In a laboratory study, Morgan-Short et al., (2014) used measures of procedural learning ability to predict individual differences in L2 syntactic development at early and late stages of acquisition under implicit training conditions that included comprehension and production practice. This condition exposed fourteen participants to an artificial L2 (Brocanto2) without grammatical explanations or instructions to search for rules. Participants had to use the artificial L2 for comprehension and production in the context of a computer-based game board. The two measures of procedural learning ability used were a dual-task version of the Weather Prediction task and the Tower of London task. The study hypothesized a positive relationship between declarative learning ability and early L2 syntactic development, and a positive relationship between procedural memory ability and late L2 syntactic development. The results provided support to the hypothesis. In the initial stages of syntactic development (i.e., after learners completed twelve practice modules), declarative learning ability correlated with learning outcomes as measured by a grammaticality judgment test. Specifically, the MLAT-V subtest of paired associates showed a significant positive correlation. In later stages of syntactic development (i.e., after learners completed seventy-two practice modules), it was procedural learning ability that showed a relationship with learning outcomes. In this case, both the Weather Prediction and the Tower of London tasks showed significant correlations. These results indicated that declarative and procedural learning abilities predict L2 syntactic development differentially. In the early stages of acquisition, learning can occur quickly, relying on the declarative memory system, whereas, in later stages, learning proceeds gradually through repeated exposure, relying on the procedural memory system. Learners with an advantage at declarative learning ability may need minimal exposure to form declarative memory about the language. On the other hand, learners with an advantage at procedural learning ability may do better when they are given the opportunity of additional training and exposure.

A follow-up study by Morgan-Short et al. (2015) used neuroimaging techniques to provide further evidence about L2 learners' reliance on different memory systems during the acquisition of syntax. The study looked at the neural representation of L2 syntax in the brain under an implicit training context and whether these neural circuits differed among learners with different levels of performance on declarative and procedural learning ability tasks. The results showed that neural activity while answering to the grammaticality judgment test was not related to individual differences in procedural memory ability at the early stage of syntactic development, but was related to individual differences in declarative memory ability. On the other hand, learners with poorer procedural memory ability obtained poorer grammaticality judgment test scores at the late stage of syntactic development and showed increased levels of neural activation while answering to the grammaticality judgment test. This suggests that learners with poorer procedural memory ability required more effortful, and therefore less efficient, neural recruitment levels.

In another laboratory study, Brooks, Kwoka, and Kempe (2017) investigated whether statistical learning ability, among other cognitive abilities, facilitated learning and generalization of L2 morphology of a miniature Russian case-marking paradigm under two input conditions. One input condition included a balanced and, therefore, more predictable, distribution of morphological cases, whereas the other input condition included a skewed and, therefore, less predictable distribution. The study tested whether less predictable input would facilitate learning. Participants were fifty-four college-level students in the United States with zero knowledge of Russian and Slavic languages. The study used an auditory artificial grammar learning task to assess statistical learning ability. The task, from Misyak and Christiansen (2012), included auditory sequences of nonwords that followed a series of production. After listening to the nonword sequences, participants were asked to complete a test that presented pairs of sequences, one that followed the same rules as the input they had been exposed to and one that did not. The results showed that the auditory artificial grammar learning task was a significant predictor of accuracy in comprehension and a significant predictor of accuracy in production, but only for old items (novel items showing generalization of learning were predicted by nonverbal intelligence with the mediation of participants' explicit awareness).

In a similar study, Hamrick (2015) investigated whether individual differences in declarative and/or procedural memory abilities predicted learning of novel syntactic structures in a semi-artificial language paradigm under incidental conditions. In this paradigm, words in English (participants' native language) are placed into the syntactic structures of another language, in this case a language adapted from Persian, in order to avoid the need for vocabulary pre-training and minimize intentional learning by focusing participants' attention on meaning comprehension of scrambled sentences. The SRT task was used as a measure of procedural memory ability. The results showed that immediate recognition task scores were significantly correlated with declarative memory ability (measured in the study using the LLAMA-B subtest), but not with procedural memory ability, while delayed recognition task scores showed the reverse pattern, that is to say, they were significantly correlated with procedural memory ability, but not with declarative memory ability. This result suggested a relationship between procedural memory ability and the retention of incidentally learned L2 syntax after a period of one to three weeks of no exposure. That is to say, after a period of no exposure, procedural memory mechanisms started supporting L2 syntax abilities. However, as Hamrick points out, these findings should be interpreted with caution, since delayed recognition task scores were not significantly above zero, according to one-sample *t*-tests. In addition, the study could have suffered from lack of power, due to the small number of participants who completed all the tests ($n = 18$).

Granena and Yilmaz (2019a) also used a SRT task, in this case as a measure of implicit learning ability, in order to investigate whether it moderated the effectiveness of two feedback interventions, implicit via recasts and explicit via explicit correction. The study focused on two structures in Spanish, gender agreement and direct object marking, and used a self-paced reading task to measure learning gains. Self-paced reading measures online sensitivity to language errors while participants read sentences for comprehension and it is considered a more fine-grained measure of implicit language knowledge (Vafaee, Suzuki, & Kachinske, 2017). A total of seventy-nine college-level learners of Spanish in the United States participated in the study. The results showed a significant relationship between implicit sequence learning ability and sensitivity to feminine gender agreement errors on the posttest in the implicit feedback group only. This means that those learners with greater implicit learning ability became more sensitive to feminine gender agreement violations after receiving implicit feedback. However, the fact that posttest sensitivity scores in the implicit feedback group were not statistically different from the scores in explicit or control groups warrants caution in interpreting these results. While changes in sensitivity in the implicit feedback group could not be confidently attributed to the feedback treatment provided, Granena and Yilmaz (2019a) reported statistically significant pre-to-post development in degree of sensitivity in the implicit feedback group associated with a large effect size. The study concluded that implicit learning ability could be predicting the acquisition of grammatical agreement, since grammatical agreement, like statistical learning, involves co-occurrence patterns within utterances and transitional probabilities, that is, the probability of one event given the occurrence of another event.

Like the studies in naturalistic learning contexts, the studies that have investigated implicit language aptitude in instructed contexts have mostly focused on the SRT task as a measure of implicit learning ability. They have shown that individual differences in SRT task performance are meaningfully related to L2 learning outcomes under certain instructional conditions and, therefore, that this research is clearly warranted. Although the empirical evidence of implicit learning in instructed contexts to date is slim (see Paciorek & Williams, 2015), theoretically, the argument has been made that implicit processes are the default mode for L2 learning (Doughty, 2003; Long, 2014) and that they are necessary for language learning at advanced levels (Ellis, 2005). Therefore, there is a need to continue investigating implicit L2 learning in laboratory settings and in the language classroom using designs that incorporate the effect of individual differences in implicit cognitive abilities as measured by multiple tasks and stimuli in different modalities.

4 What Are the Implications for SLA and Pedagogy?

The notion of implicit language aptitude has major implications for SLA theory and practice. At a theoretical level, aptitude research can provide indirect evidence of the type of cognitive processes responsible for learning outcomes on different language features, in different age-of-onset groups, or under different instructional interventions (see DeKeyser, 2012). A positive association between a cognitive factor and learning under a specific condition indirectly means that the mental processes that are engaged by the instructional condition are facilitated by the value of the learner's specific cognitive ability. This is where a distinction between cognitive abilities for explicit and implicit learning can be especially relevant since we can obtain indirect evidence that learners were drawing on explicit or implicit cognitive processes when learning under a particular condition. This evidence can be further triangulated with more direct types of evidence of the mental processes learners engaged in during learning, for example, via think-aloud protocols, which could be easily incorporated to text-based computer-mediated communication via text chat.

At a practical level, the notion of an aptitude for implicit language learning is meaningful in language learning contexts, whether naturalistic, study abroad, or instructed where experiential approaches, such as task-based language teaching, are followed. In these contexts, implicit learning and processing can happen, since the capacity for implicit learning may weaken, but does not disappear in adulthood, as argued in Section 1 of this Element.[3] The connection between implicit language aptitude and language learning may not be transparent because aptitude reflects potential for learning, or a deficit that reduces potential for learning. In addition, learners have no evidence of the cognitive abilities they are drawing on while acquiring the L2. However, the relationship between individual differences in implicit cognitive abilities and L2 instruction can become apparent by matching type of instruction, or pedagogical intervention, to the learners' cognitive profile. This requires building hypotheses regarding the relationship between implicit language aptitude and L2 learning. For example, a learner with a higher primability score will have better listening comprehension skills, will find it easier to access related words, and will be able to automatically build meaning associations between words. Then, in order to gain maximum benefit from an instructional practice, a pedagogic intervention can be designed that matches the learners' cognitive strengths. For example, a pedagogic intervention for a learner with a high primability score could include longer, authentic texts and spoken passages and could focus on building vocabulary through authentic materials.

A recent study that investigated the effects of matching and mismatching aptitude profile with type of instruction on L2 learning outcomes was Granena and Yilmaz (2019b). In the study, L2 learners with a high explicit–low implicit aptitude profile and L2 learners with a low explicit–high implicit aptitude profile were compared under two instructional interventions that matched and mismatched each of the profiles (explicit and implicit corrective feedback). Differentiated instruction appeared to work in the predicted direction for most of the comparisons. The matched profile outperformed the mismatched profile at a descriptive level. Despite the descriptive trends observed, many of the comparisons did not reach statistical significance and, given the small sample sizes in each of the profiles, the results of the study were at most tentative. We are still far from being able to generalize findings from studies involving implicit cognitive abilities and implicit learning conditions, largely because of

---

[3] An anonymous reviewer questioned the relevance of implicit cognitive abilities to instructed SLA on the grounds that input and output, whether provided by teachers or other learners, have to be explicitly noticed, with awareness, for learning to occur. According to the same reviewer, gradual speed-up of already acquired knowledge, unlike learning, could happen without awareness.

the lack of instructed SLA studies that include both factors (i.e., implicit cognitive abilities and implicit instruction) as part of the same design. However, aptitude-treatment interaction (ATI) research in the field of educational psychology has shown that it is possible to optimize learning by adapting teaching practices to individual characteristics. Although differentiation as educational practice may be difficult to implement in face-to-face contexts, it is highly promising for online adaptive language learning contexts because of the possibility to customize and systematically match learners to particular instructional modules after determining their cognitive strengths.

5 What Are the New Avenues for Research?

There are two main avenues for future research on implicit language aptitude where work is clearly needed:

1. Research on the reliability and construct validity of implicit learning and memory tasks
2. Research on interactions between implicit language aptitude and different instructional interventions, different language features or different starting ages of L2 learning

Research is needed that investigates the construct validity of implicit language aptitude by means of factor analyses and/or structural equation models that test the underlying structure of a variety of implicit learning and implicit memory tasks. A unitary, or general, ability of implicit learning has not been supported in the literature. It is possible that it exists, but it is also possible that there are multiple, even unrelated, forms of implicit learning (Seger, 1994). Two major experimental paradigms of implicit learning, artificial grammar learning and SRT, shared no common variance in studies such as Gebauer and Mackintosh (2007) and Kalra et al. (2019). Factors such as modality (visual/auditory) and stimulus specificities (verbal/nonverbal, natural/synthesized speech, exposure duration) may be placing different constraints on performance resulting in variation in individuals' sensitivity across modalities and stimuli. For example, Conway and Christiansen (2005) reported significant differences in sequence learning in different modalities (tactile, visual, and auditory). Further research should use a broad sample of learning and memory tasks to explore the structure of individual differences in implicit language aptitude.

Research is also needed that investigates the reliability of implicit learning and memory tasks and their stability over time as individual capacities. Measures of reliability include a large enough variance of scores, test–retest reliability (i.e., reliability over time), and split-half reliability and Cronbach's alpha as internal reliability and consistency. Compared to explicit cognitive measures, which rely on overall performance, implicit tasks tend to be noisier because they rely on difference scores and, as a result, show lower reliability indices (Cronbach, 1970). Granena (2013a) reported a reliability of 0.44 for a probabilistic serial reaction time task, using split-halves with Spearman-Brown correction. Kaufman et al. (2010) also reported a reliability of 0.44 and considered it standard for probabilistic SRT tasks, on the basis of the reliability of implicit learning in the literature (Dienes, 1992; Reber et al., 1991; Robinson, 1997). Reber et al. (1991) and Robinson's (1997) replication study reported split-half reliabilities of 0.51 and 0.52, respectively, also using the Spearman-Brown correction. Statistical learning tasks (e.g., Newport & Aslin, 2004) even had reliabilities of 0.23 and 0.31. These values stand in sharp contrast with those reported for standard cognitive tests, typically 0.70 or higher. Low reliability does not undermine the validity of a task in assessing implicit learning, but it casts doubts on its potential efficiency as a predictor. In other words, reliability is a property of the scores of a measure (i.e., it is sample-dependent), rather than the measure itself, and, if low, it compromises the predictive validity of the scores.

While low reliability indices are a cause for concern, not all implicit measures have low reliability. Kalra et al. (2019), for instance, reported moderate test–retest reliability indices for a serial reaction time task, a category-learning task, and a probabilistic classification task. Research should identify the most reliable tasks and find ways to increase the reliability of assessment for the construct. As Woltz (2003) suggests, imposing greater constraints on performance for a task will increase reliability. For example, one option is to set specific performance goals and avoid multiple solutions for an item, since these can involve different cognitive processes.

The second avenue for research is ATI studies. There are few SLA studies that have investigated implicit cognitive abilities in either naturalistic or instructed language learning contexts. Interactions between implicit language aptitude and different instructional interventions, different language structures, or different starting ages of L2 learning can provide indirect evidence of the nature of the learning processes involved in L2 outcomes (DeKeyser, 2012). The interaction between implicit language aptitude and instructional treatment, the one with the most practical importance, has been the most researched so far, but it has been largely limited to studies where the SRT task has been used as a measure of implicit language aptitude. The interaction that has been less researched so far has been the interaction between implicit language aptitude and target structure. As DeKeyser (2012) suggests, this interaction can show how different language aspects are learned through different mechanisms. Structures differ in terms of their salience or their complexity and this can make them more sensitive to age effects or more difficult to acquire. Understanding the learning processes at work during their acquisition would have considerable theoretical and practical implications. Finally, a last interaction that is also theoretically and practically important is the interaction between implicit language aptitude and starting age of L2 learning. This is an interaction that has been relatively well investigated in relation to explicit language aptitude and cognitive abilities such as verbal analytical ability. However, the research that has looked at more implicit cognitive abilities is scarce. Naturalistic, or immersion, contexts provide an optimal learning environment to investigate potential relationships between implicit language aptitude and L2 learning outcomes by learners who started learning the L2 early in childhood or later as adults. This environment maximizes the opportunities for implicit learning by providing massive input exposure in communicative situations. In this context, interaction research has the potential to show how cognitive aptitudes for implicit learning help L2 learners detect complex and noisy regularities.

6 Conclusion

The domain of implicit cognition is a complex domain, with constructs that do not necessarily overlap. A main distinction that can be made is between implicit learning and implicit memory. Both have been proposed in this section as the two main constituents of implicit language aptitude. When researchers study implicit learning they typically focus on encoding, the first stage of memory where information is acquired and consolidated. The notion of implicit learning in the Reberian sense is coextensive with the notion of procedural memory acquisition, except when procedural memory acquisition is understood following Anderson's (1987) conception of skill learning, which allows for initial explicit learning. Implicit memory, on the other hand, refers to the maintenance and retrieval stage, the process of recalling stored information. The type of implicit memory ability discussed in this Element has been primability, or priming ability. Both implicit learning and implicit memory can be measured using different tasks, different modalities, and different types of stimuli. Therefore, research is needed to understand the extent to which these tasks are measuring a common construct, as well as research into ways to increase the reliability of assessment of the construct. This would advance the SLA field in understanding the promise of implicit language aptitude as a theoretical construct and its suitability to measure individual differences from a psychometric perspective. Only when the predictive validity of implicit language aptitude is not questioned, will researchers be able to confidently use it as a predictor to explain variation in L2 learning outcomes. As in any new area of research, there are still more questions than answers, but the few studies available and their findings suggest that further research is warranted.

References

Anderson, J. R. (1987). Skill acquisition: Compilation of weak-method problem solutions. *Psychological Review*, *94*, 192–210.

Batterink, L., Reber, P. J., Neville, H. J., & Paller, K. A. (2015). Implicit and explicit contributions to statistical learning. *Journal of Memory and Language*, *83*, 62–78.

Berry, D. C., & Dienes, Z. (1993). *Implicit learning: Theoretical and empirical issues*. Hove, UK: Erlbaum.

Bertels, J., Franco, A., & Destrebecqz, A. (2012). How implicit is visual statistical learning? *Journal of Experimental Psychology: Learning, Memory, and Cognition*, *38*, 1425–1431.

Bley-Vroman, R. (1990). The logical problem of foreign language learning. *Linguistic Analysis*, *20*, 3–49.

Bley-Vroman, R. (2009). The evolving context of the fundamental difference hypothesis. *Studies in Second Language Acquisition*, *31*, 175–198.

Brooks, P. J., Kwoka, N., & Kempe, V. (2017). Distributional effects and individual differences in L2 morphology learning. *Language Learning*, *67*, 171–207.

Carroll, J. B. (1958). A factor analysis of two foreign language aptitude batteries. *Journal of General Psychology*, *59*, 3–9.

Carroll, J. B. (1962). The prediction of success in intensive foreign language training. In R. Glaser (ed.), *Training research and education* (pp. 87–136). Pittsburgh: University of Pittsburgh Press.

Carroll, J. B. (1981). Twenty-five years of research in foreign language aptitude. In K. Diller (ed.), *Individual differences and universals in language learning aptitude* (pp. 83–118). Rowley, MA: Newbury House.

Carroll, J. B., & Sapon, S. (1959). *Modern Language Aptitude Test: Form A*. New York: Psychological Corporation.

Chan, C. (1992). Implicit cognitive processes: Theoretical issues and applications in computer systems design. Unpublished doctoral dissertation. University of Oxford.

Cheesman, J., & Merikle, P. M. (1984). Priming with and without awareness. *Perception & Psychophysics*, *36*, 387–395.

Chomsky, N. (1965). *Aspects of the theory of syntax*. Oxford, UK: MIT Press.

Cleeremans, A., Allakhverdov, V., & Kuvaldina, M. (2019). Introduction. In A. Cleeremans, V. Allakhverdov, & M. Kuvaldina (eds.), *Implicit learning: 50 years on* (pp. 1–15). London: Routledge.

Cleeremans, A., Destrebecqz, A., & Boyer, M. (1998). Implicit learning: News from the front. *Trends in Cognitive Sciences, 2*, 406–416.

Conway, C. M., & Christiansen, M. H. (2005). Modality-constrained statistical learning of tactile, visual, and auditory sequences. *Journal of Experimental Psychology: Learning, Memory, and Cognition, 31*, 24–39.

Conway, C. M., Bauernschmidt, A., Huang, S. S., & Pisoni, D. B. (2010). Implicit statistical learning in language processing: Word predictability is the key. *Cognition, 114*, 356–371.

Costa, P. T., Jr., & McCrae, R. R. (1992). Four ways five factors are basic. *Personality and Individual Differences, 13*, 653–665.

Cronbach, L. J. (1970). *Essentials of psychological testing* (3rd ed.). New York: Harper & Row.

Cronbach, L. J., & Snow, R. E. (1977). *Aptitudes and instructional methods: A handbook for research on interactions*. New York: Irvington.

Defense Language Institute Foreign Language Center. (2009). *Defense language proficiency testing system: Familiarization guide*. www.dliflc.edu/wp-content/uploads/2014/04/DLPT-IV_Fam-guide-for-Web-based-test.pdf.

DeKeyser, R. M. (2000). The robustness of critical period effects in second language acquisition. *Studies in Second Language Acquisition, 22*, 499–533.

DeKeyser, R. (2007). Skill acquisition theory. In B. VanPatten & J. Williams (eds.), *Theories in second language acquisition: An introduction* (pp. 97–112). Mahwah, NJ: Erlbaum.

DeKeyser, R. M. (2012). Interactions between individual differences, treatments, and structures in SLA. *Language Learning, 62*, 189–200.

DeKeyser, R. M., & Koeth, T. (2011). Cognitive aptitudes for second language learning. In E. Hinkel (ed.), *Handbook of research in second language teaching and learning* (Vol. 2, pp. 395–406). London: Routledge.

Dennis, N. A., Howard, J. H., & Howard, D. V. (2006). Implicit sequence learning without motor sequencing in young and old adults. *Experimental Brain Research, 175*, 153–164.

Destrebecqz, A., & Cleeremans, A. (2001). Can sequence learning be implicit? New evidence with the process dissociation procedure. *Psychonomic Bulletin and Review, 8*, 343–350.

DeYoung, C. G., Quilty, L. C., & Peterson, J. B. (2007). Between facets and domains: 10 aspects of the Big Five. *Journal of Personality and Social Psychology, 93*, 880–896.

Dienes, Z. (1992). Connectionist and memory array models of artificial grammar learning. *Cognitive Science, 16*, 41–79.

Dienes, Z., & Perner, J. (1999). A theory of implicit and explicit knowledge. *Behavioral and Brain Sciences, 22*, 735–755.

Dienes, Z., Altmann, G., Kwan, L., & Goode, A. (1995). Unconscious knowledge of artificial grammars is applied strategically. *Journal of Experimental Psychology: Learning, Memory, & Cognition, 21*, 1322–1338.

Doughty, C. J. (2003). Instructed SLA: Constraints, compensation, and enhancement. In C. J. Doughty & M. H. Long (eds.), *Handbook of Second Language Acquisition* (pp. 256–310). Oxford: Blackwell Publishers.

Doughty, C. J., Campbell, S. G., Mislevy, M. A., et al. (2010). Predicting near-native ability: The factor structure and reliability of Hi-LAB. In M. T. Prior, Y. Watanabe, & S-K. Lee (eds.), *Selected proceedings of the 2008 Second Language Research Forum* (pp. 10–31). Somerville, MA: Cascadilla Proceedings Project.

Dulany, D. E., Carlson, A., & Dewey, G. I. (1984). A case of syntactical learning and judgment: How conscious and how abstract? *Journal of Experimental Psychology: General, 113*, 541–555.

Ellis, N. C. (1996). Sequencing in SLA: Phonological memory, chunking and points of order. *Studies in Second Language Acquisition, 18*, 91–126.

Ellis, N. C. (2005). At the interface: Dynamic interactions of explicit and implicit language knowledge. *Studies in Second Language Acquisition, 27*, 305–352.

Ellis, N. C., & Cadierno, T. (2009). Constructing a second language. *Annual Review of Cognitive Linguistics, 7*, 111–139.

Emberson, L. L., Conway, C. M., & Christiansen, M. H. (2011). Timing is everything: Changes in presentation rate have opposite effects on auditory and visual implicit statistical learning. *The Quarterly Journal of Experimental Psychology, 64*, 1021–1040.

Epstein, S. (1990). Cognitive–experiential self-theory. In L. Pervin (ed.), *Handbook of personality theory and research* (pp. 165–192). New York: Guilford Press.

Epstein, S. (1994). Integration of the cognitive and the psychodynamic unconscious. *American Psychologist, 49*, 709–724.

Epstein, S. (2008). Intuition from the perspective of cognitive–experiential self-theory. In H. Plessner, C. Betsch, & T. Betsch (eds.), *Intuition in judgment and decision making* (pp. 23–37). New York: Erlbaum.

Evans, J. S. B. T., & Over, D. E. (1996). *Rationality and reasoning*. Hove: Psychology Press.

Feldman, J., Kerr, B., & Streissguth, A. P. (1995). Correlational analyses of procedural and declarative learning performance. *Intelligence, 20*, 87–114.

Foerde, K., Knowlton, B.J., & Poldrack, R.A. (2006). Modulation of competing memory systems by distraction. *Proceedings of the National Academy of Sciences, 103*, 11778–11783.

Franco, A., Eberlen, J., Destrebecqz, A., Cleeremans, A., & Bertels, J. (2015). Rapid serial auditory presentation: A new measure of statistical learning in speech segmentation. *Experimental Psychology, 62*, 346–351.

Fried, L. S., & Holyoak, K. J. (1984). Induction of category distributions: A framework for classification learning. *Journal of Experimental Psychology: Learning, Memory, and Cognition, 10*, 234–257.

Frost, R., Siegelman, N., Narkiss, A., & Afek, L. (2013). What predicts successful literacy acquisition in a second language? *Psychological Science, 24*, 1243–1252.

Gangopadhyay, I. McDonald, M., Ellis Weismer, S., & Kaushanskaya, M. (2018). Planning abilities in bilingual and monolingual children: Role of verbal mediation and inhibitory control. *Frontiers in Psychology, 9*, 323.

Gebauer, G. F. (2003). Implicit learning and intelligence. Unpublished doctoral dissertation. University of Cambridge.

Gebauer, G. F., & Mackintosh, N. J. (2007). Psychometric intelligence dissociates implicit and explicit learning. *Journal of Experimental Psychology, 33*, 34–54.

Glicksohn, A., & Cohen, A. (2013). The role of cross-modal associations in statistical learning. *Psychonomic Bulletin & Review, 20*, 1161–1169.

Gluck, M., Shohamy, D., & Myers, C. (2002). How do people solve the "weather prediction" task? Individual variability in strategies for probabilistic category learning. *Learning & Memory, 9*, 408–418.

Graf, P., Mandler, G., & Haden, M. (1982). Simulating amnesic symptoms in normal subjects. *Science, 218*, 1243–1244.

Granena, G. (2013a). Cognitive aptitudes for second language learning and the LLAMA Language Aptitude Test. In G. Granena & M. H. Long (eds.), *Sensitive periods, language aptitude, and ultimate L2 attainment* (pp. 105–129). Amsterdam: John Benjamins.

Granena, G. (2013b). Individual differences in sequence learning ability and SLA in early childhood and adulthood. *Language Learning, 63*, 665–703.

Granena, G. (2016). Cognitive aptitudes for implicit and explicit learning and information-processing styles: An individual differences study. *Applied Psycholinguistics, 37*, 577–600.

Granena, G. (2019). Cognitive aptitudes and L2 speaking proficiency: Links between LLAMA and Hi-LAB. *Studies in Second Language Acquisition, 41*, 313–336.

Granena, G., & Yilmaz, Y. (2019a). Corrective feedback and the role of implicit sequence learning ability in L2 online performance. *Language Learning, 69*, S1, 127–156.

Granena, G., & Yilmaz, Y. (2019b). Language aptitude profiles and the effectiveness of implicit and explicit corrective feedback. In R. Leow (ed.), *The Routledge handbook of second language research in classroom learning* (pp. 438–451). New York: Routledge.

Gupta, P., & Cohen, N. J. (2002). Theoretical and computational analysis of skill learning, repetition priming, and procedural memory. *Psychological Review, 109*, 401–448.

Hamrick, P. (2015). Declarative and procedural memory abilities as individual differences in incidental language learning. *Learning and Individual Differences, 44*, 9–15.

Heindel, W. C., Festa, E. K., Ott, B. R., Landy, K., & Salmon, D. P. (2013). Prototype learning and dissociable categorization systems in Alzheimer's disease. *Neuropsychologia, 51*, 1699–1708.

Howard, J. H., Jr., & Howard D. V. (1997). Age differences in implicit learning of higher order dependencies in serial patterns. *Psychology and Aging, 12*, 634–656.

Hoyer, W. J., & Lincourt, A. E. (1998). Ageing and the development of learning. In Stadler, M. A., & Frensch, P. A. (eds.), *Handbook of implicit learning* (pp. 445–470). Thousand Oaks: Sage.

Hulstijn, J. H. (2005). Theoretical and empirical issues in the study of implicit and explicit second-language learning. *Studies in Second Language Acquisition, 27*, 129–140.

Jacoby, L. L., & Dallas, M. (1981). On the relationship between autobiographical memory and perceptual learning. *Journal of Experimental Psychology: General, 110*, 306–340.

Janacsek, K., Fiser, J., & Nemeth, D. (2012). The best time to acquire new skills: Age-related differences in implicit sequence learning across the human lifespan. *Developmental Science, 15*, 496–505.

Jimenez, L. (2002). Attention in probabilistic sequence learning. In L. Jimenez (ed.), *Attention and implicit learning* (pp. 43–67). Amsterdam: John Benjamins.

Kalra, P. (2015). Implicit learning: Development, individual differences, and educational implications. Unpublished doctoral dissertation. Harvard University.

Kalra, P., Gabrieli, J. D. E., & Finn, A. S. (2019). Evidence of stable individual differences in implicit learning. *Cognition, 190*, 199–211.

Kaufman, S., DeYoung, C., Gray, J., Jiménez, L., Brown, J., & Mackintosh, N. (2010). Implicit learning as an ability. *Cognition, 116*, 321–340.

Keri, S. (2003). The cognitive neuroscience of category learning. *Brain Research Reviews, 43*, 85–109.

Kim, K., & Godfroid, A. (2019). Individual differences in cognitive aptitudes and implicit-explicit knowledge: An SEM approach. Paper presented at the American Association of Applied Linguistics annual conference, Atlanta, GA.

Kirkham, N. Z., Slemmer, J. A., & Johnson, S. P. (2002). Visual statistical learning in infancy: Evidence for a domain general learning mechanism. *Cognition*, *83*, B35–B42.

Knowlton, B., Squire, L. R., & Gluck, M. A. (1994). Probabilistic classification in amnesia. *Learning and Memory*, *1*, 106–120.

Knowlton, B. J., Mangels, J. A., & Squire, L. R. (1996). A neostriatal habit learning system in humans. *Science*, *273*, 1399–1402.

Knowlton, B. J., Siegel, A. L., & Moody, T. D. (2017). Procedural learning in humans. In J. H. Byrne (ed.), *Learning and memory: A comprehensive reference* (pp. 295–312). Oxford: Academic Press.

Linck, J. R., Hughes, M. M., Campbell, S. G., et al. (2013). Hi-LAB: A new measure of aptitude for high-level language proficiency. *Language Learning*, *63*, 530–566.

Long, M. H. (2014). *Second language acquisition and task-based language teaching*. Malden, MA: Wiley-Blackwell.

Long, M. H. (2017). Instructed second language acquisition (ISLA): Geopolitics, methodological issues, and some major research questions. *Instructed Second Language Acquisition*, *1*, 7–44.

Long, M. H., & Doughty, C. (2009). *The Handbook of language teaching*. Malden, MA: Wiley-Blackwell.

MacDonald, K. B. (2008). Effortful control, explicit processing, and the regulation of human evolved predispositions. *Psychological Review*, *115*, 1012–1031.

Maie, R. (2019). Demystifying the complexity of individual differences under incidental conditions: A conceptual replication and extension. Paper presented at the American Association of Applied Linguistics annual conference, Atlanta, GA.

Marslen-Wilson, W., & Tyler, L. (1980). The temporal structure of spoken language processing. *Cognition*, *8*, 1–71.

McGeorge, P., Crawford, J. R., & Kelly, S. W. (1997). The relationships between psychometric intelligence and learning in an explicit and an implicit task. *Journal of Experimental Psychology: Learning, Memory, and Cognition*, *23*, 239–245.

Meara, P. (2005). *LLAMA language aptitude tests*. Swansea, UK: Lognostics.

Meisel, J. (2009). Second language acquisition in early childhood. *Zeitschrift für Sprachwissenschaft*, *28*, 5–34.

Misyak, J., & Christiansen, M. (2012). Statistical learning and language: An individual differences study. *Language Learning*, *62*, 302–331.

Morgan-Short, K., Faretta-Stutenberg, M., Brill-Schuetz, K., Carpenter, H., & Wong, P.C.M. (2014). Declarative and procedural memory as individual differences in second language acquisition. *Bilingualism: Language and Cognition*, *17*, 56–72.

Morgan-Short, K., Faretta-Stutenberg, M., & Bartlett-Hsu, L. (2015). Contribution of event-related potential research into explicit and implicit second language acquisition. In P. Rebuschat (ed.), *Investigating implicit and explicit language learning* (pp. 349–386). Amsterdam: John Benjamins.

Myers, I., McCaulley, M. H., Quenk, N. L., & Hammer, A. L. (1998). *Manual: A guide to the development and use of the Myers–Briggs Type Indicator* (2nd ed.). Palo Alto, CA: Consulting Psychologists Press.

Newport, E. L., & Aslin, R. N. (2004). Learning at a distance: I. Statistical learning of nonadjacent dependencies. *Cognitive Psychology*, *48*, 127–162.

Nissen, M. J., & Bullemer, P. (1987). Attentional requirements of learning: evidence from performance measures. *Cognitive Psychology*, *19*, 1–32.

Pacini, R., & Epstein, S. (1999). The relation of rational and experiential information processing styles to personality, basic beliefs, and the ratio-bias phenomenon. *Journal of Personality and Social Psychology*, *76*, 972–987.

Paciorek, A., & Williams, J. N. (2015). Implicit learning of semantic preferences of verbs. *Studies in Second Language Acquisition*, *37*, 359–382.

Peretti, C. H., Danion, J. M., Gierski, F., Grange, D. (2002). Cognitive skill learning and aging. A component process analysis. *Archives of Clinical Neuropsychology*, *17*, 445–459.

Petersen, C. & Al-Haik, A. (1976). The development of the Defense Language Aptitude Battery (DLAB). *Educational and Psychological Measurement*, *36*, 369–380.

Phillips, L. H., Wynn, V., Gilhooly, K. J., Della Sala, S., & Logie, R. H. (1999). The role of memory in the Tower of London task. *Memory*, *7*, 209–231.

Pimsleur, P. (1966). *Pimsleur Language Aptitude Battery (PLAB)*. New York: Psychological Corporation.

Poldrack, R. A., & Gabrieli, J. D. E. (2001). Characterizing the neural mechanisms of skill learning and repetition priming: Evidence from mirror-reading. *Brain*, *124*, 67–82.

Pretz, J. E., Totz, K. S., & Kaufman, S. B. (2010). The effects of mood, cognitive style, and cognitive ability on implicit learning. *Learning and Individual Differences*, *20*, 215–219.

Price, A. L. (2009). Distinguishing the contributions of implicit and explicit processes to performance of the weather prediction task. *Memory and Cognition, 37*, 210–222.

Ranta, L. (2008). Aptitude and good language learners. In C. Griffiths (ed.), *Lessons from good language learners* (pp. 142–154). Cambridge: Cambridge University Press.

Reber, A. S. (1967). Implicit learning of artificial grammars. *Journal of Verbal Learning and Verbal Behavior, 6*, 855–863.

Reber, A. S. (1969). Transfer of syntactic structure in synthetic languages. *Journal of Experimental Psychology, 81*, 115–119.

Reber, A. S. (1989). Implicit learning and tacit knowledge. *Journal of Experimental Psychology General, 118*, 219–235.

Reber, A. S. (1993). *Implicit learning and tacit knowledge: An essay on the cognitive unconscious.* London: Oxford University Press.

Reber, A. S., & Allen, R. (2000). Individual differences in implicit learning: Implications for the evolution of consciousness. In R. G. Kunzendorf & B. Wallace (eds.), *Individual differences in conscious experience* (Vol. 20, pp. 227–247). Amsterdam: John Benjamins.

Reber, A. S., & Millward, R. B. (1965). Event memory in probability learning. *Psychonomic Science, 3*, 431–432.

Reber, A. S., & Millward, R. B. (1968). Event observation in probability learning. *Journal of Experimental Psychology, 77*, 317–327.

Reber, A. S., Walkenfeld, F., & Hernstadt, R. (1991). Implicit and explicit learning: Individual differences and IQ. *Journal of Experimental Psychology: Learning, Memory, and Cognition, 17*, 888–896.

Reber, P., Gitelman, D., Parrish, T., & Mesulam, M. (2003). Dissociating explicit and implicit category knowledge with fMRI. *Journal of Cognitive Neuroscience, 15*, 574–583.

Rebuschat, P. (2008). Implicit learning of natural language syntax. Unpublished doctoral dissertation. University of Cambridge.

Rebuschat, P. & Williams, J. N. (2006). Dissociating implicit and explicit learning of natural language syntax. In R. Sun & N. Miyake (eds.) *Proceedings of the annual meeting of the Cognitive Science Society*, p. 2594. Mahwah, NJ: Lawrence Erlbaum.

Rebuschat, P. & Williams, J. N. (2009). Implicit learning of word order. In N. A. Taatgen & H. van Rijn (eds.), *Proceedings of the 31th annual conference of the Cognitive Science Society* (pp. 425–430). Austin, TX: Cognitive Science Society.

Reed, J., & Johnson, P. (1994). Assessing implicit learning with indirect tests: Determining what is learned about sequence structure. *Journal of Experimental Psychology: Learning, Memory, and Cognition, 20,* 585–594.

Robinson, P. (1997). Individual differences and the fundamental similarity of implicit and explicit adult second language learning. *Language Learning, 47,* 45–99.

Robinson, P. (2005). Cognitive abilities, chunk-strength, and frequency effects in implicit artificial grammar and incidental L2 learning: Replications of Reber, Walkenfeld, and Hernstadt (1991) and Knowlton and Squire (1996) and their relevance for SLA. *Studies in Second Language Acquisition, 27,* 235–268.

Saffran, J. R., Newport, E. L., Aslin, R. N., Tunick, R. A., and Barrueco, S. (1997). Incidental language learning. *Psychological Science, 8,* 101–105.

Saint-Cyr J. A., Taylor A. E., Lang A. E. (1988). Procedural learning and neostriatal dysfunction in man. *Brain, 111,* 941–959.

Schacter, D. L. (1987). Implicit memory: History and current status. *Journal of Experimental Psychology: Learning, Memory, and Cognition, 13,* 501–518.

Schacter, D. L., & Graf, P. (1986). Effects of elaborative processing on implicit and explicit memory for new associations. *Journal of Experimental Psychology: Learning, Memory, and Cognition, 12,* 432–444.

Seger, C. A. (1994). Implicit learning. *Psychological Bulletin, 115,* 163–196.

Shallice, T. (1982). Specific impairments of planning. *Philosophical Transactions of the Royal Society of London, 298,* 199–209.

Shanks, D. R., & Johnstone, T. (1999). Evaluating the relationship between explicit and implicit knowledge in a serial reaction time task. *Journal of Experimental Psychology: Learning, Memory, & Cognition, 25,* 1435–1451.

Siegelman, N., & Frost, R. (2015). Statistical learning as an individual ability: Theoretical perspectives and empirical evidence. *Journal of Memory and Language, 81,* 105–120.

Siegelman, N., Bogaerts, L., & Frost, R. (2016). Measuring individual differences in statistical learning: Current pitfalls and possible solutions. *Behavior Research Methods, 49,* 1–15.

Siegelman, N., Bogaerts, L., Elazar, A., Arciuli, J., & Frost, R. (2018). Linguistic entrenchment: Prior knowledge impacts statistical learning performance. *Cognition, 177,* 198–213.

Simon, H. A. (1975). The functional equivalence of problem solving skills. *Cognitive Psychology, 7,* 268–288.

Skehan, P. (1989). *Individual differences in second language learning.* London: Arnold.

Snow, R. E. (1991). Aptitude-treatment-interaction as a framework for research on individual differences in psychotherapy. *Journal of Consulting and Clinical Psychology, 59,* 205–216.

Squire, L. R. (1987). *Memory and brain*. New York: Oxford University Press.

Squire, L. R. (1992). Memory and the hippocampus: a synthesis from findings with rats, monkeys, and humans. *Psychological Review, 99*, 195–231.

Squire, L. R., & Zola-Morgan, S. (1991). The medial temporal lobe memory system. *Science, 253*, 1380–1386.

Squire, L. R., Knowlton, B. & Musen, G. (1993). The structure and organization of memory. *Annual Review of Psychology, 44*, 453–495.

Stanovich, K. E., & West, R. F. (2000). Individual differences in reasoning: Implications for the rationality debate? *Behavioral and Brain Sciences, 23*, 645–665.

Stansfield, C., & Winke, P. (2008). Testing language aptitude. In E. Shohamy & N. H. Hornberger (eds.), *Encyclopedia of language and education: Language testing and assessment* (2nd ed., Vol. 7, pp. 81–94). New York: Springer.

Suzuki, Y., & DeKeyser, R. M. (2015). Comparing elicited imitation and word monitoring as measures of implicit knowledge. *Language Learning, 65*, 860–895.

Suzuki, Y., & DeKeyser, R. M. (2017). The interface of explicit and implicit knowledge in a second language: Insights from individual differences in cognitive aptitudes. *Language Learning, 67*, 747–790.

Thakral, P. P., Kensinger, E. A., & Slotnick, S. D. (2016). Familiarity and priming are mediated by overlapping neural substrates. *Brain Research, 1632*, 107–118.

Tunney, R. J., & Shanks, D. R. (2003). Subjective measures of awareness and implicit cognition. *Memory & Cognition, 31*, 1060–1071.

Turk-Browne, N. B., Junge, J. A., & Scholl, B. J. (2005). The automaticity of visual statistical learning. *Journal of Experimental Psychology-General, 134*, 552–564.

Unsworth, N., & Engle, R. W. (2005a). Individual differences in working memory capacity and learning: Evidence from the serial reaction time task. *Memory & Cognition, 33*, 213–220.

Vafaee, P., Suzuki, Y., & Kachinske, I. (2017). Validating grammaticality judgment tests: Evidence from two new psycholinguistic measures. *Studies in Second Language Acquisition, 39*, 59–95.

Wang W. C., & Yonelinas, A. P. (2012). Familiarity is related to conceptual implicit memory: An examination of individual differences. *Psychonomic Bulletin & Review, 19*, 1154–1164.

Was, C. A., & Woltz, D. J. (2007). Reexamining the relationship between working memory and comprehension: The role of available long-term memory. *Journal of Memory and Language, 56*, 86–102.

Williams, J. N. (1999). Memory, attention, and inductive learning. *Studies in Second Language Acquisition, 21*, 1–48.

Williams, J. N. (2005). Learning without awareness. *Studies in Second Language Acquisition, 27*, 269–304.

Willingham, D. B., Nissen, M. J., & Bullemer, P. (1989). On the development of procedural and declarative knowledge. *Journal of Experimental Psychology: Learning, Memory, and Cognition, 15*, 1047–1060.

Winter, B., & Reber, A. S. (1994). Implicit learning and natural language acquisition. In N.C. Ellis (ed.), *Implicit and explicit learning of languages* (pp. 115–146). London: Academic Press.

Witteman, C., van den Bercken, J., Claes, L., & Godoy, A. (2009). Assessing rational and intuitive thinking styles. *European Journal of Psychological Assessment, 25*, 39–47.

Woltz, D. J. (1990a). Decay of repetition priming effects and its relation to retention from text processing: A study of forgetting. *Learning and Individual Differences, 2*, 241–261.

Woltz, D. J. (1990b). Repetition of semantic comparisons: Temporary and persistent priming effects. *Journal of Experimental Psychology: Learning, Memory, and Cognition, 16*, 392–403.

Woltz, D. J. (1999). Individual differences in priming: The roles of implicit facilitation from prior processing. In P. L. Ackerman, P. C. Kyllonen,& R. D. Roberts (eds.), *Learning and individual differences: Process, trait, and content determinants* (pp. 135–156). Washington, DC: American Psychological Association.

Woltz, D. J. (2003). Implicit cognitive processes as aptitudes for learning. *Educational Psychologist, 38*, 95–104.

Woolhouse, L., & Bayne, R. (2000). Personality and the use of intuition: Individual differences in strategy and performance on an implicit learning task. *European Journal of Personality, 14*, 157–169.

Yonelinas, A. P. (2002). The nature of recollection and familiarity: A review of 30 years of research. *Journal of Memory and Language, 46*, 441–517.

Zaki, S. R., Nosofsky, R. M., Jessup, N. M., & Unverzagt, F. W. (2003). Categorization and recognition performance of a memory-impaired group: Evidence for single system models. *Journal of the International Neuropsychological Society, 9*, 394–406.

Cambridge Elements ≡

Second Language Acquisition

Alessandro Benati

The University of Hong Kong

Alessandro Benati is Professor of English and Applied Linguistics at the American University of Sharjah (UAE). He is internationally known for his research in second language acquisition and ground-breaking work on Processing Instruction. He has authored research monographs and articles in high-impact journals, including *Second Language Research* and *Language Teaching*. Alessandro is a member of AHRC Peer Review College, REF 2021, and honorary professor at the York St John University and the University of Portsmouth.

John W. Schwieter

Wilfrid Laurier University, Ontario

John W. Schwieter is Associate Professor of Spanish and Linguistics, and Faculty of Arts Teaching Scholar, at Wilfrid Laurier University. His research interests include psycholinguistic and neurolinguistic approaches to multilingualism and language acquisition; second language teaching and learning; translation and cognition; and language, culture, and society.

About the Series

Second Language Acquisition showcases a high-quality set of updatable, concise works that address how learners come to internalize the linguistic system of another language and how they make use of that linguistic system. Contributions reflect the interdisciplinary nature of the field, drawing on theories, hypotheses, and frameworks from education, linguistics, psychology, and neurology, among other disciplines. Each Element in this series addresses several important questions: What are the key concepts?; What are the main branches of research?; What are the implications for SLA?; What are the implications for pedagogy?; What are the new avenues for research?; and What are the key readings?

Cambridge Elements $\equiv$

Second Language Acquisition

Elements in the Series

Proficiency Predictors in Sequential Bilinguals
Lynette Austin, Arturo E. Hernandez and John W. Schwieter

Implicit Language Aptitude
Gisela Granena

A full series listing is available at: www.cambridge.org/esla

Printed in the United States
By Bookmasters